Bob wrote this Manuscript in the 1980s. So some of his references are now dated.

Bob was guilty of the Murder of both his father and mother.

The courts found that he was "insane" at the time but he was confined in Gaol "at the Governor's Pleasure".

This is the true story, told by him of his time in prison and of his eventual release into "Freedom", and more importantly, of his Redemption.

I must thank the Mother of God Brothers, who did not really know me or what kind of a person I was on the inside, but still put a lot of trust in me and took me at FACE VALUE and lived out the Gospel according to Christ's word in so doing. But I appreciate that they did something here for me that was entirely out of human charity. That is not a very common thing in a world that lives by grabbing everything for itself, and where the law of the jungle and the animal kingdom seems to reign supreme.

I also have to thank my friend, Dr Paul Lush, and the people of Albury themselves who have been friendly to me since my coming to live here.

Last of all, I wish to thank my dear cousin, Fay, for never giving up on me after what I did, but she stuck staunchly by me. She truly proved that blood is thicker than water and showed the essence of true Christian love. Her love for me must be greater than I deserve.

Bob Cox and Denis Devcich

THE BOB COX STORY

AUSTIN MACAULEY PUBLISHERS™
LONDON • CAMBRIDGE • NEW YORK • SHARJAH

Copyright © Bob Cox and Denis Devcich 2023

The right of Bob Cox and Denis Devcich to be identified as authors of this work has been asserted by the authors in accordance with sections 77 and 78 of the Copyright, Designs and Patents Act 1988.

All rights reserved. No part of this publication may be reproduced, stored in a retrieval system, or transmitted in any form or by any means, electronic, mechanical, photocopying, recording, or otherwise, without the prior permission of the publishers.

Any person who commits any unauthorised act in relation to this publication may be liable to criminal prosecution and civil claims for damages.

All of the events in this memoir are true to the best of author's memory. The views expressed in this memoir are solely those of the author.

A CIP catalogue record for this title is available from the British Library.

ISBN 9781398459076 (Paperback)
ISBN 9781398459083 (ePub e-book)

www.austinmacauley.com

First Published 2023
Austin Macauley Publishers Ltd®
1 Canada Square
Canary Wharf
London
E14 5AA

I wish to acknowledge the great grace given to me by God Almighty. I thank my Saviour, Our Lord, Jesus Christ, who enabled me to be open to the grace of the Holy Spirit to begin to make amends for my failures. I am grateful to Our Lady, the Blessed Virgin Mary and Mother of God, for the guidance she gave to enable me to embrace the "Truth that sets all humanity free".

Table of Contents

Introduction   11
    My Family   *11*
    Grandma's Place   *15*

The Trams   **20**
    The Leather Jacket   *22*
    A Disturbing Influence?   *24*
    The Easter Show   *28*
    Toenails   *31*

The Beginning of the End or the End of the Beginning   **35**
    The Murders   *35*
    Long Bay Gaol   *38*

Food   **49**
    Goulburn Gaol   *52*
    The Tailor's Shop   *57*
    The Captain   *64*
    "Batman"   *65*

"The Winger"	*67*
The Bulgarian	*69*
The "Riot at Goulburn"	*72*
(Such as it was.)	*72*
Parramatta Gaol	*79*
BIBLE?	*83*
The Slot Thief	**90**
New Guys	*94*
The Teacup	*98*
Changes	*103*
Shoplifting – a five year setback	*107*
Freedom?	*113*
"Institutionalisation Syndrome"	*115*
Postscript	**117**

Introduction

I am adding this introductory section of my life so as to make the whole thing as complete as possible. The early years of my life that I spent at home with my friends and my parents, my early school life and my years of growing up, which for a long time made me extremely happy, but later on the despair at being a part of a world that offered no objective or goal, the thought of marriage and a family did not seem a realistic future for me. I was too much of a stormtrooper for such a course of domestic day by day drudgery.

****

My Family

I was born on the 21st day of September in the year 1942. There must have been something a bit more exciting going on somewhere in the world at the time when my dear mother saw fit to bring me into the world. Anyway I was born in the Newtown District Maternity Hospital.

My earliest memories at home are living in the flat that my parents rented, which was one of four built from this extremely old house, with a large brick wall and hedge around it. It occupied the corner of Liverpool Road and Cobden Street at Enfield in the Western Suburbs of Sydney. I think it had been a doctor's house or maybe even a small hospital. But then the owner has bricked up doorways here and there and made it into the four flats. Our flat was nice. It had a front and back door, the only one of the four, now I recall, that did.

It was nice, not in the image of the new modern block style flat you get nowadays, but because it was well kept and clean, and neat and spotless right throughout. I've got to hand it to my mother Dell. She was a tireless house-keeper. In those years before lots of people owned electrical conveniences, she would get down on her hands and knees and wax the kitchen floor. She would do all the washing in the old gas copper. For years she never even had a washing machine, she got a vacuum cleaner after a while, and of course if me and my father or uncle or anybody else were home, we would chip in and help her all we could.

My father was a good, honest and hardworking man. He would get drunk sometimes, mostly only on pay night, or sometimes on Saturday after he had had a winning day at the races. He didn't always win of course, but he must have got a good tip, somewhere off somebody, at times, because on occasions he would give my mum a big roll of five-pound notes, which she would take to the bank, and use to buy us things that we needed badly. But punting wasn't always a big deal with my Pop and he had the good common sense to give it away before it got the best of him.

My mum didn't mind my dad drinking beer, after work and sometimes she would join him in a bottle or two in the hot weather on his "pay night". She (my mother) would not, however, agree to him bringing wine into the house; she was very severe on this subject. It had a very bad "Jekyll and Hyde" intoxicating effect on my dad, and if she caught him with a bottle in the house, she would very promptly and unhesitatingly smash it down the nearest outside drain that she could find. I think that deep down inside my father knew just how right she was about this subject.

Anyway, apart from minor upsets, my home life was pretty normal and being an only child they saw that I was always as well off as the most well cared for of children. I suppose I have the good Lord above to thank for that.

I wasn't too much for thinking much about God in those times. My dad never brought the subject up, but my mother must have been brought up to be god-fearing, because of a night she would kneel in bed and say her prayers.

She (my mum) insisted on sending me to Sunday School. So I tried this one and that one, and different ones around the local area. I had friends, usually sons of some particular neighbours or somebody like this, who would agree to take me usually. Well, like I say, it wasn't all so bad, this Sunday School business, but I somehow used to find myself taking more notice of the little spunkies (girls) that used to go than of the religious lessons. But as it turned out, I must have been a bit slow, and more of a looker than a doer, because I never had a serious girlfriend, until I was well into my teens. Most of my friends were in this same category as well.

I used to think I was pretty tough in my own mind I suppose. But if I knew some street kid who was tougher than me, then I would still try to befriend him, and for the most part, it usually paid off, and I was pretty well liked, I think by most of the guys and respected too, among my friends. Of course there are always that section of the juvenile underworld who are too far removed, unapproachable – so to speak. Usually these guys think that they are some considerable amount tougher than you are, and that you are not good (tough) enough to mix with them or join their clique (that's what they think!).

So I grew up with this kind of subconscious belief that I was some kind of lone gunslinger or tough gangland hood, but I never told anybody this, or bragged about this – you understand the whole thing was a state of mind – I even had this inward belief that I was the reincarnated spirit of all the great *Outlaw* killers right from Billy the Kid, to Jessie James and Babyface Nelson and guys like this. Tough guys and Gangsters, Rebels against the man-made laws of society. These were the guys who I hero worshipped, and looked up to. Well I suppose people would think that this train of thought is childish and rather stupid, but is it? So much? I mean the world is rough, and tough. You only had to grow up in my neighbourhood, to realise this. In one's childhood, and in the school yard, at lunchtime and even in the classrooms of adolescent youth, this is where the budding "heavies" of society get their lessons in life, and this is where the very first lessons in love, sex, spite, hatred, extortion, greed and the good old biff and 'stand over' are firstly introduced. So with this realisation taken into mind, was my attitude so much to be condemned or wondered at?

Despite this, I never carried brass knuckles or knives on my person, and neither did my friends. Like I previously stated, we were all Sunday School dropouts, reasonably polite kids, with some schooling in Christian ideals.

Well, I got through primary school with a reasonably sound education, and was sent from there to the old Cleveland Street High School in the city. It used to only be an Intermediate High School, but now (the year that I started), it had been made into a full five-year Leaving Certificate High School.

We would usually go and stay at my grandma's place up at West Wallsend, near Newcastle, on my school holidays.

If my dad could get his holidays from work, simultaneously (which quite often he would), he would be able to come too!

Grandma's Place

My grandmother lived out on the Lake Road where it was mostly all bush at this time. It was about two houses down from the Reservoir Road branch off.

The guy who had the house on the corner of Reservoir Road, and who was my grandma's next door neighbour, was someone I will call Ernie Emm, who I didn't like very much, and this was because I got the strong impression that he didn't like me, and that, in turn, was because his good looking spunky wife Audrey, did like me, and would make a fuss of me, and even hug and kiss me sometimes (of course I was pretty young at this time). Anyway the more Audrey would dote over me, the more jealous, 'stupid bloody Ernie' would become, and the more I would lap it up, and hang around her, and so on.

Gees! She was some smasher of luscious doll, that Audrey. Too bad she was so much older than me, and that she was married to such a 'dickhead' as Ernie.

My grandparents' house was called Hallsville, the word was painted in big letters on the front. It was a nice old country place, built very solid, all of brick, with a fruit orchard and flower gardens and vegetable patches and a vacant playing field and trellises, where passion-fruits grew aplenty all the way around, It also lots of chooks and they even had two milking cows for a long time, and my grandpa or grandma would do the separating and sell (or keep) the cream and home-made butter.

It was all a city boy like myself could want, and my growing up years there were very happy.

My grandma and grandpa had several children all grown up (my aunt and uncles). My mum, Dell, had only one sister (Heather) and all the rest were boys. There was Matthew, the eldest and Eric. Then there was Walter, who served in the Great War, and came home. Then there was Gus who I have heard it said, was my grandma's favourite, maybe they just said it because Gus (Augustus Brockwell Hall) was killed somewhere on the field in France, anyway it was with military honours, and they gave my grandma a big, bronze medallion, which she had fixed onto a brass arch, and which held the place of honour in the lounge room. Then there was Cecil, who I had never met, maybe he was dead too, I don't know, and then my uncle Roy, and last but by no means least my uncle Sam who had properties, sheep and cattle, near Bingara and Barraba, and who was married to my aunty Amy, and whose first three boys were Benny, Bob and Don; they were at least ten years older than me.

My uncle Roy's kids were Steven and Delly. They were only older than me by a couple of years, and they led me into the use of cigarettes and grog.

Ben, Bob and Don and others would play games, parlour games, like monopoly or cards. You reckon, these games, (sometimes for money) wouldn't get involved. Some of these games used to become so heated that they would go outside and wrestle each other to see who could come out on top, and if they wrestled long and hard enough, then they used to sit down and think about how silly they'd been, and finish up by laughing about the whole thing.

Gees! It was damn funny to watch these three, and everybody used to get a kick out of their antics. They were all good horsemen too, and used to go with my uncle Eric in the bush and help him on droves and musters.

So at Christmas time, we'd have these big family reunions, and everybody would come along, and bring their family, and the whole place would be like an anthill. Everybody rushing everywhere in this door, and out this door, and in this room and out that, and doing this and doing that, and all of us kids would be gallivanting around and playing hide and seek and getting in all the grown up people's road, and so forth and so on. Also there would be a great deal of hugging and kissing and exchanging of presents and cracking open of bottles of beer and wine and scotch whisky or brandy (among the men) while the ladies and girls would be exchanging a lot of gossip and stories about their boyfriends and all this malarkey, while trying to help my grandma, who needed all the help she could get.

But my poor old grandpa would just sit in a chair, and wonder what all the fuss and commotion was that was going on around him. He knew of course, that it was the Christmas festivities; his brain was as good and agile as it ever had been, but his eyesight and hearing were nearly completely gone and when he walked, he moved extremely slowly and with the aid of a walking stick.

I didn't know what the life story behind my grandpa and grandma was, but it must have gone back a long way to the horse and gig days, before there was even any electricity or public transport.

All I knew was that they only spoke to each other on occasions, when conversation was inescapable, and that they slept in different rooms.

My grandmother was an excellent cook and would rather cook on the old fuel stove out the back in the shed, than use the new electric one that she had in the house.

Deliciously roasted turkeys and chickens with all the trimmings! It was all a great delicacy then, and something to be waited for, not like now with all the Chicken Stop places and Kentucky Fried. There were none of such places around in these earlier times and a chicken or turkey meal was something that one might work for, and wait on, from one year's end to another, especially for people who came from the Big City.

My grandmother was also a very qualified cook and made lovely Christmas cakes with hard candy icing that would nearly break your teeth and great big Christmas puddings full of wine and brandy and rum with threepenny and sixpenny pieces. You'd have to chew warily through those puddings, and then you'd bite into something hard. It was all a lot of fun, as I recall, those Christmas reunions. When we'd return to our flat in the city, it would have a musty smell. But by the following day everything would be back to normal again.

The Trams

One of the best things about growing up in those early years was travelling on the trams. School kids could travel any distance for one penny.

They used to travel all the way out to the suburbs and back again, along the old tar roads. The old tar roads in those days were full of bumps, and cars that went along them had to go slow in order that they wouldn't get shaken to pieces.

I would sit up on the footpath of the main road of an evening, and wait for my Pop (dad) to come home from work. Sooner or later, I'd see him get off the tram, with his familiar hat on, and his newspaper sticking out of his side pocket, like always. But until Pop did come I just used to sit there (sometimes with Colly, my friend) and watch all the old cars, trams and old vehicles, long since forgotten, coming down along the way.

Then sometime, at some later date, the dawn of progress intervened, and men came along on the work gangs, and all of a sudden there they were ripping the tramlines up. Well it had to be done everywhere, all over the Metropolitan area of Sydney and all the outlying suburbs, and it must have taken quite a while to do, but soon, after a while, they did it, and set about laying the foundations for the big new concrete highway that was to replace the old tar roads. And on came Double Decker Buses to replace the Trams – so much for the March of Progress.

I started at "Clevo" (the High School) just before the trams finished. We had to wear grey suits and light-grey shirts and blue-and-white ties; we also had sweaters and school socks with the blue-and-white stripes.

They tried to get us to wear hats, and they introduced a nice blue hatband, with the school crest on the front. But the hat idea was never popular and "the Shape" or "Pear-Shape" (Mr Bradley the headmaster) must have told them not to bother enforcing it, he wasn't a bad old geezer "the Shape".

Then they told us that we could purchase school blazers for about £12 (pounds) each. They were very nice and dressy, royal blue, with blue-and-white piping on the pockets and cuffs, and the school crest on the pocket. They changed the crest when the blazer came out, I always considered the old crest the best. We also had a solid brass lapel badge under which was the School Motto (Nulla Dies Sine Linia) which meant, never a day without something achieved.

Well, after I started at Clevo things started to change rapidly, weekend life was very fast. A lot faster than country folk, who were satisfied usually to lead, a rather placid, not too hectic lifestyle. But when you are a teenager growing up in the jungle of the big city, you live a pretty fast kind of life usually.

The Leather Jacket

So it was goodbye to Sunday School classes, I gave them the cold shoulder, and grabbed the old Marlon Brando Leather Jacket. Man! I doubt in those times if I would have parted with that jacket for anything. On the back were two red gates painted on top of which was a white grinning skull, and the words "gates of Hell get ready". Every kid made up his own insignia for his jacket in those days and usually did his own paint work, unless of course you knew some guy who had some special skill in this field. I must have wagged school about, at least, two days, out of every week in those years. I'd go to town, with my friends Ray and Bill, and we'd sit through session after session of movies like, *Rock around the Clock*, and *Jailhouse Rock*, or maybe we'd go and check the gear out at places like Scottish Tailoring, up in Liverpool Street that carried all the latest "very hip" gear and all the really coolest sets of threads around. We were right in style in those days. At the weekend we would make the scene at the movies with, black-and-white check sports coats, and blue birds-eye trousers, with funnel hoop belt loops, and pegged 14" or 15" cuffs. We had Ivy League shirts and Mitchell Blue and Presley Purple Sweaters, and my mum even brought me a pair of fire-engine red brogues with black shoe laces, very smart and really flash. So we'd wear all this gear at the weekend, I don' t think fashion will ever be as good as it was then, in the days of *Bandstand* and *Six O'clock Rock* etc. The original "Rock 'n' Roll" years!

Still, despite all these good times and seemingly endless enjoyment and late-night parties – at different guys' houses where I would get invited and sometimes meet some nice girl that I never had known before – still despite all of this, there was still this deep psychological nagging in the back of my mind, where something kept asking me, where are you going after this, and what! Another day to do the same old boring things? Where is this world heading? Anywhere? Is there any real purpose in life for you, Bob? I don't think that my friends used to worry about the future the same way that I did, but for me, it presented this constant problem. I know now, that my parents both loved me very much, after all I was their only begotten son, and it hurts me immensely now when I stop to think of how much I must have hurt them, and all the heartbreak that they must have felt, seeing me becoming so cold and unapproachable as I did, day by day, in those times and for no apparent reason.

I can remember from the newspapers things that made big news and world history in those years. Like the crossing of the 38th Parallel that heralded the start of the Korean War and the Chinese Communist Revolution under Chairman Mao, the Hungarian Occupation, the disappearance of Harold Holt and the assassination of John F. Kennedy. I left school and had jobs. I took a salesman job in the city for a while as a tool salesman behind the counter at the two stores and the bulk store of a big Sydney Tool Retailer. I also had a job as a fireman on the Steam Engines.

Before I left school, I had to repeat third year in order to get my Intermediate Certificate. My mother had her heart set on this. So I tried real hard, for her sake, to pass this exam, and eventually did, well you couldn't accuse me of being entirely illiterate. An Intermediate Certificate was *no end of help*, when it came to finding a job in those days. Still I did get the impression that they just about gave it to me to get rid of me, to stop me from hanging around for yet another year.

A Disturbing Influence?

I can see how I may very well have been a disturbing influence on the kids who were coming up to my level. Without really trying too hard, I used to get a lot of laughs from these younger guys. Not that I was trying to disrupt them, you understand. These younger kids just have the habit of looking up to other older guys (even though it may only be a year or so difference) with an aspect of awe and respect due to their more experienced position in the class. Even the damned teachers seemed to get a tickle out of me for some reason. I reckon maybe it was my good "poker face" that used to get them all going.

Maybe I should have gone and seen Bobby Limb or Bob Dyer or somebody in those days about a job as a comedian; I may have finished up as a big hit on current TV. If I had done that and liked the life, well who knows what might have happened?

But quite frankly, when I looked in the mirror, I couldn't see a particularly funny guy – no! My thoughts were all too much of a serious nature, to be regarded as funny. I didn't know what I was going to do; I didn't want to be an ordinary, run-of-the-mill bludger. I didn't want to be a millstone around my parents' neck. I couldn't foresee the events of the Vietnam conflict, and the future didn't seem to offer any promise for this 'first rate action guy' and 'leader of men' that I saw myself as. I do not wish to sound too vain or imaginative at this point, but all things taken into consideration, including the type of guy I mostly was, well, I could very well have made a good Master Sergeant. If the US Army had come out to Australia to draught conscripts for the US Army, "Master Sergeant Cox", that does seem to have a realistic ring to it "n'est pas"? I imagined being a teacher of jungle survival and unarmed combat and veteran, with CMH (Congressional Medal of Honour) and Purple Heart and more fruit salad on my uniform than you could poke a stick at. Yeah! I can see it all now! I probably would have done my parents proud by having my picture on the front of TIME magazine or something. Too bad it never really happened. My uncle Jack objected. He was my dad's younger brother (his proper name was Sylvan Ellyton Ordell Cox – that's a mouthful for most people) – my uncle Jack didn't like his given name apparently, I don't know why. I suppose it did have a bit of a "pooffy" ring about it, so in his young Air Force days they used to call him "Bub" or "Jack". So Jack used to be a bomber pilot in the RAAF and flew a few bombing missions over New Guinea when the Japs were making their presence felt there, from all I could gather.

After that (now) Uncle Jack came and lived with us. My dad wasn't in the war, he was able to serve better by using his skills as a qualified fitter and turner to help make torpedo parts and submarine fittings at a large engineering firm "Arnolds Pty Ltd".

I've seen old photos of the types of lathes my dad used to operate; they were huge. The whole lathe was about as long as a submarine and everything turning and spinning at a tremendous rate. No thanks, I'd rather take my chances against the Japs. Later on, my dad did lose the top half of three of his fingers in a lathe accident.

Jack was a great joker, a funny bloke who most people would get a real tickle from. He was always the life of the party, and all that! My uncle Eric's daughter Fay, my first cousin, came and lived with us in those early years, long before she thought of getting married. I loved Fay then and still do, even now. She was always more like a sister to me than a cousin and nothing was too good for me, in her estimation. I remember once that I was sitting at the table and when the meal was over, I couldn't resist just walking around and planting a great big kiss fair on her neck. She started to blush, but she didn't mind by all accounts. I couldn't help it, I just had to kiss her like that! She was beautiful, and I was her favourite. Fay had a couple of particular boyfriends. The first one I remember was Vince H. I was only young at this time, probably about four or five, but I remember Vince well. He had real red hair and would carry me on his shoulders, or throw me into the air and catch me (thank goodness) and all stuff like this, a real nice likeable bloke. He was an "A Grade" Rugby League player, and when Fay wasn't going to see him play, well he would be taking her out to see somebody else play. I think all this great love of Rugby League of Vince's must have been the ruination of their companionship because after a while she dropped him – (broke off the relationship sounds a bit better).

Then there was Gill B. He was a big, I suppose you would have to describe him as handsome and athletic as well as quiet and shy kind of a fellow. He was so damned quiet and shy, Fay would say, when telling my mum about some date they had, or something, that she (Fay) would feel like kicking poor old Gill in the shins. Poor old Gill, he was a poor inoffensive kind of "poor bastard", but he used to worship Fay, that was for sure.

He certainly had a crush on her, and would always be mooching around the house (our place) trying to see her. My Pop (and Jack) would get pretty "pissed off" because every time you'd look around there would be old Gill, on the doorstep waiting to see Fay. No wonder it was that he never got over her when she told him that it was all over between them. I remember she used to say that after work sometimes, she would still see Gill following her around. She must have dropped Gill after she met Eric – Eric James. She finally got married to Eric, a flash and very smart little guy, about the same height as her. Eric was an X-ray operator at St Vincent's Hospital in Sydney.

Later after they had been married for some time, he took on a salesman's job, selling and demonstrating Volkswagen cars for one of the biggest dealers of these cars in the city!

Like I said he was a cluey smart kind of little guy able to turn his hand to anything with a fair amount of success. He took up scuba diving, and even made his own underwater camera.

When he was a youth, he had been a scout and even held the rank of "Kings Scout", or nowadays it would be of course, "Queens Scout" and that's about as high as you can get as a scout, without actually being a Scoutmaster. But even lots of Scout-masters wouldn't have the awards and merits that it takes to be a "Queens Scout".

The Easter Show

My Pop used to take me to the Easter Show about every year in those years when I was really young. We'd walk around everywhere and look at all the exhibitions, and he'd buy me lots of show bags. In those days the show bags only used to cost a bob or two to buy, and you'd get lots of nice little samples – and things to play with like puzzles and lollies galore in great big packets, and goodness knows what else. One of the bags, the Minty Bag used to even give you a punch out, rubber operated Zip gun that would fire cardboard pellets. Then you'd get all the small sample jars of mustard and Hot Sauce and Tomato Sauce, and peanut butter and Vegemite and Baked Beans and all stuff like this that you could eat or keep till later but that was very useful, not so much useless rubbish as you get nowadays.

The model railway exhibition put on by the New South Wales Railway was very good, and had all the ins and outs of a real railway with Sheds and pits and signals and turntables and tunnels and Stations, just like a real railway. They'd have about six full length trains going and stopping for signals, and going into sidings and so forth and so on, – you could stand there and watch them for hours.

The Police Exhibition would draw a lot of people, and was kind of interesting in a grotesque macabre and horrifying kind of way. The first thing you'd see immediately on your right hand side when entering the doorway of the exhibition, was the big life size figure of Ned Kelly in full armour with his pistol in his hand and his foot up on a log. Then after that there were photos and pictures of the rest of the Kelly Gang – Steve

Hart, Joe Byrne and Ned's brother Dan. Large mug shots, photographs of their faces mainly in wooden frames.

Also in the light with their actual firearms under each of them were the framed photos of such desperadoes as Morgan, Moonlight, Capt. Thunderbolt and Jackey Jackey. Ben Hall's gang of Ben Hall, O'Mally, Gilbert and Dunn were not forgotten, also lit up and holding positions of honour and distinction in this rogues gallery.

Then there were murder displays of gruesome, but intriguing calibre such as the human glove, taken from the disgorged arm in the Shark Arm case and the death mask and photos of the face and burnt and mutilated body of the pyjama girl, Linda Agostini and the weapon, a hammer, that was used in this most publicised case.

Then as you would move down along the rail there were all these exhibits of automatic pistols, lady's handbag guns and derringers. revolvers and other weapons such as knives, bludgeons, hammers and various unnameable weapons used in a vast array of extremely brutal and macabre murders. There was also a big sign in red lettering block letters on a white board, which said, "Please do not touch the exhibits".

The next exhibits were more photos of Underworld figures such as Squizzy Tailor and Frankie Green (the little Gunman) and famous call girls that came to violent deaths, such as "Pretty" Dulcie and Shirley Butler, under which would be printed information on these people, very informative and a great glimpse into the more realistic side (if you like) of those early days of Australian life, and how these desperate men and women lived.

(There was more to the Police Exhibition then, I cannot try to describe the whole lot).

And so forth and so on. There were the side shows that used to get all the attention and that have long since faded into memory, like the Wall of Death and Jimmy Sharmen's Boxing Troupe and the Country and Western shows like the LeGarde. Twins and Chad Morgan and Slim Dusty and Rock and Rollers like Laurel Lea and Dig Richards and the Delltones, etc. And the big gigantic rubber balloons had this funny stinky Easter Show smell about them that was familiar to that particular place only.

Jack certainly loved his food and sometimes we would be lying in bed on a Saturday morning (I had my own bed and room of course). Anyway I would hear Jack up in the kitchen fussin' around, and preparing something he had brought home from Paddy's Markets. Then all of a sudden he would come in and try and shovel a great big spoonful of Tasmanian Scallops in parsley sauce, or Toheroa Soup or curried tripe or whatever down your throat while you would be lying there, and say, "Here get this into you" or "Try this for size and you'll sleep on bags" or something like this.

He also had a bad habit of trying to get my dad to drink bottled beer before breakfast. This did not strike a particularly acceptable chord with my mum, who would get "off her bike" good and proper, so Jack got the message and didn't do it after that. He didn't want to "stir" my mum up too much!

Most of the people in our street were Protestant as were my mother and father, but not particularly bigoted ones or even church going ones, and my mum and dad had some good Catholic friends in our street, John, Anne and Noel Armstrong, I knew them well. My mother was close friends with June their mother, and Ron, their father was a friendly enough bloke who would always give us a friendly greeting if he saw us in the back yard, while walking past. I knew that my father and Jack were Masons. I didn't know what the Catholic Church stood for, I hadn't even bothered to find out, I wasn't really religious at all, and if I believed in anything in those times. I suppose it would have to be reincarnation or something of this notion.

This damned Masonic Business was shrouded in mystery. Some blokes in our street were always going to lodge meetings, you'd see them trotting up the street with their black tuxedos on and their little black bags in their hands. I never ever saw my dad or Jack attend a meeting so maybe they had thought about it all again and decided that they didn't agree with it because, like I say, they never went to a meeting that I ever saw or witnessed.

Paddy Ryan who lived down the street on the corner was a "Micky" (Roman Catholic) also and so was Tommy Hamer the local Butcher who my parents had been friends with for a long, long time and who invited my parents and Jack to their daughter Joan's wedding ceremony and reception.

Toenails

Our landlord "Old Frosty" or just "Frosty" to my mother and father, lived in the front flat. He was a self-confessed Atheist, and used to work as a chemist at Park Davis & Co. He had been to India in his earlier years, and his job had also taken him to the United States at least twice. He had two sons Col and Valiant. Colly was two years younger than me and Val was two years older. Colly was my very best friend in those years at home, and I had a lot of respect for Val because he was older and a good sportsperson, and was good fun to talk to. Colly was born normal intellectually but had a hair lip. Val was normal and had reddish ginger hair. They were very good neighbours, the Frosts. "Frosty's" name was Valiant Lynton Frost (Senior). His wife's name was "Rae".

She was Jewish and a very, very nice person.

"Frosty" owned an "Oldsmobile", which he used to park in the gravel driveway. He may have attained it while in the USA. I couldn't know for sure about that, but they used to often take me for an outing in it at the weekends (before my grandpa died and we became financial enough to buy our own car) and we would drive way out across Tom Ugly's Bridge, and stop and boil the Billy or cook Frankfurt's.

We had these other people who we would quite frequently go and stay with, in my younger years. They came from up around my father's old hunting ground around Cundletown, that's just a few miles out of Taree, right on the bank of the Manning River. These friends went back to long before I could remember – before I was even born, they were related to my dad somewhere along the line. These people were the Gills – Bert who owned the only butchery in Cundle, and Maude (Auntie Maude); she was about as old as my grandma Hall, "real old" in other words. Bert and Maude had three children, all grown up and about middle aged with children, except Doreen. Doreen had never got married. Doreen was a nice, plump domestic kind of a big girl who liked to go to church on Sundays and sing hymns to God, and bake cakes and cook and help Aunty Maude as much as she could the rest of the time. Deb was the eldest and was married to Laura Cahill of the "fishing" Cahills who made their living by fishing every day. Laura herself had quite a reputation as a very good fisherwoman with a rod. Well, Deb and Laura had a dairy farm just out of Cundle and two children about the same age (a bit younger) than yours truly. Judith and John. I think I must have been in love with Judith, and I even think that maybe she might have felt the same way towards me. But we were too young, and she was too cautious about city boys to give me much of a tumble, but I never forgot Judith. She did have a lovely, healthy body and personality.

Bert's youngest son was Dallas who, like his father, was the one to carry on the butchering business, and had the slaughterhouse on his property which ran spillways down into the river (a tributary to the Manning). The countryside was "raked all over" with these smaller tributaries, all of which are teeming with beautiful fish. Well anyway Dallas lived there with his wife Marie (I don't know what her family name was), but she was a nice pleasant, laughing kind of person too, and rather pretty too, I might add, she used to make a big fuss of me. Dallas was always "too busy to talk much". He used to be always busy at the slaughterhouse, or seeing that the sausages were being made properly. Gill's sausages had a very proud reputation around Cundle and the Taree area. Old Bert still worked, though, he still managed "Gill's Butchery" the shop in Cundle, and drove the delivery truck sometimes. He was a real old, funny kind of man, Bert was, with a grey pipe, stained moustache and glasses.

I don't know if Bert ever used to cut his toenails, but sometimes we'd be sitting out the back on the porch, and after he had taken his shoes off, maybe it would be Jack who would speak up and say, "God Almighty, Bert, why don't you cut those damned toenails".

To which Bert would reply after a spell, "Eh! What's that, Boy? I can't hear you! Speak up!" He used to call everyone "Boy"! But he really was getting a bit deaf, he had a hearing aid. Then at last after my Pop and Jack had shouted at him for about five minutes, then he'd say "Oh! So you think I should cut these toenails eh? Well I did! Just the other day". This would just about kill my Pop who would laugh at Bert sometimes till his eyes would fill up with tears. He would laugh so much. Finally he (Bert) would get the scissors and set about doing it after everyone in the whole house (including Auntie Maude) had nagged him enough about it. (It was just one great big joke with Bert, he'd purposely hang off doing it (cutting his toenails) for as long a spell as possible. (I don't know how long that this spell would be) just to annoy everybody. Even Dallas, who probably had a stronger stomach than most people, would be appalled at the way Bert would let his toenails grow for ages on end. After tea and then to finish up I would have to do it for him. I felt I was obliged to do it. The lot fell to me anyway. But for years thereafter the subject of Bert's toenails could be a topic of ponderous debate, from anyone who had known this great old guy.

The Beginning of the End or the End of the Beginning

Well you know what I had said before about myself growing extremely cold and unapproachable over the adolescent years of my youth towards my mum and dad. Well, this increased and got worse and worse till at this particular stage I had been studying books about Hitler and the SS and the days of the Hitler Youth and the methods of the Gestapo and so forth and so on. Well, I had myself psyched so intently in this manner of absolute inhumanity towards my fellow person, well I must have been a bloody vegetable, that's all I can surmise it as.

The Murders

Well like I have said, I had myself psyched up real good, at this stage, and at this stage of the story, (and my life) it is hard to recall the events exactly – and even harder to write them down on paper. But it is necessary to this documentation that I should try hard and that these necessary details should be recorded. My father had two shotguns in the house, as a rule, one was Jack's and the other one was his.

They were both English (Cashmore 12 gauge) hunting guns of the twin, cock back hammer style, double barrelled – really good guns – to an enthusiast.

My dad had lent his gun to a workmate to hunt with. The other gun was wrapped up in pieces (disassembled) and lay in a big parcel tied with string in the corner of the wardrobe, all oiled and tied up in thick layers of newspaper and tied with string, it had been there for a long time.

I knew that the remaining one was there, so one afternoon, at the weekend, when everyone had gone out, I decided that I would assemble the gun and that I would saw down the barrel, to make a short, concealable weapon out of it. I didn't know exactly what for at this stage. But it would have to seem that even then, cold calculated murder (for that is what it was) was brewing in the back of my mind, and had taken most of all normal reasoning from my senses. This and my despair that I had no direct cause and purpose in life at this critical time had made me bent on some course of desperate confrontation, and I decided there one night after a brief argument that I should do this very wicked thing to make my mum and dad the ultimate object of my frustration.

It wasn't easy, and it isn't easy now, while I am trying to recall these things again and write them down – well, anyway I had the gun cleaned and loaded, and my parents had left the table and made their way into the bedroom. (They must have been talking about me probably). Well (God forgive me now while I think about it). I went inside, with the gun all loaded and cocked and· fronted my dad (Ainslie Walter Glenroy Cox). I fronted him with the weapon, I bailed him up, and I knew, by the non-committal expression he had, that he knew, that I wasn't kidding. He didn't laugh, and he didn't back up, an inch, or try to take the gun from me. He just stared straight at me (Jesus, you are God and I know you have forgiven me for what I did). My mum made some pretty stupid comment like. "You know something, I'm not a bit scared", or something like this, maybe she thought I was bluffing. Something in my mind said to me, "Son, you are on a one way street and there can be no turning back now" and then some computerised voice in my brain said at the same time, "Now! Do it! Now!"

Well I had the gun levelled at Dad's chest, and I pulled the trigger hard, like a killer would do it, like Baby Face Nelson or John Dillinger would have done it, that's how I did it, hard. There could be no backdowns or questions in my mind. Well that's all it took, who knows how much strength it takes to make a killer. The same strength that it took to hold the *Queen Elizabeth* or the *Queen Mary* to their moorings, the same strength that it took to drive in the final bolt that joined the Harbour Bridge from north to south. I don't know. All I know is I did it. It's over, finished, but not quite. Then, the smell of death, silence, the silence of death, present, there – in that room – inside me – I was death. The rest was automatic. Mum started screaming loudly, madly, out of control. I chased her into the lounge room and held her and shot her once, with the second barrel – she fell down, and I knew it was all over, finished. Something said to me to make sure with Mum, I had to be sure you understand that they had both gone to God, or into Eternity or whatever, but I had to be sure, that they were together. Mum was still breathing, I loaded up again, just one more round, and fired it into her chest. (God almighty! What a mess.) Now what to do? Clean the barrels out of the shotgun, nice and clean, with a pull through, just like Baby Face Nelson or John Dillinger would do, that's what! Stay cool, man, it's all over now.

Now, I've told it just like it happened. There's other brief details, but I've written down everything that matters.

I didn't give myself up, but I went and told Val Frost that I had done it.

Well the law came and arrested me later and took me down to the Burwood Station House where they photographed me and fingerprinted me – and took a statement from me and charged me with a double murder.

Well they held the inquest at the Burwood Courthouse, after which I was sent back to the Bay (Long Bay Gaol) to wait on remand, for trial to come up.

Long Bay Gaol

I must have thought at this stage that Fay or someone would come to my aid and try to bail me out. However, Eric James, Fay's husband was there, and I remember that he said that Jack had been there (at the Station House) and had left after saying to Eric that if he had his way I would never be set free again. I didn't blame him for feeling like that, poor guy. But I did get word that Jack had been killed, not that very long after in a taxi accident.

So much for the hand of fate.

Like I said there before, after the inquest I spent the night in the lockup there at Burwood, and the next morning they slapped the bracelets on my wrists, locked me in the back of the "Bun" Wagon, and I was off to Long Bay early that bleak morning along with two or three other wagons, probably from

Central, and we all rolled one after another through the front entrance of the CIP (Central Industrial Prison) and emptied their contents onto the courtyard, near the reception room, and the front gate. We all stood alongside by side on the yellow line. The head reception Screw was a lanky guy, "a three striper", he moved along the line of crims, all of us guys with "raps" ranging from vagrancy all the way to "double murder" – and relieved us of our handcuffs from whence we were ushered into the reception room, where the chief reception clerk (also a screw) seated at a desk just inside the door, took our names and descriptions and fingerprinted our index fingers (the full set of which had already been taken by the police). (By the way, every worker in a gaol was called a 'screw' by us inmates.) Then they put our "civvy clothes" away on the racks for that purpose, and our private property and valuables away in a big safe. Then we were issued with a set of underwear, and a faded pair of blue denim trousers and jacket on which was stitched our classification number. Mine was 14 I am pretty sure, anyway it was a special low number given to somebody who had to be kept under special survcillance (in the OBS which stood for Observation). This was a small section into which all felons on remand for any capital crime, e.g. murder, rape, manslaughter etc., were placed to wait for their trial to come up.

So, I left the reception room and was led by a warder across the asphalt courtyard, which also housed the "front yards" for hard to manage and intractable prisoners. They were small yards, by comparison to the ordinary ones. No 1- 18. Then there was the kitchen block "slap bang" in the middle and on each side of it more bars and a gate leading through the main section of the Prison.

The whole of Long Bay at this particular time consisted of the CIP (Central Industrial Prison) and the MRP (Metropolitan Reception Prison). This latter section was the "Long Bay" remand centre – at this time, built in one great big circle. It had previously been the old Long Bay Women's Section of the Prison.

Now there were two kinds of cell blocks, the Wings and the Ranges. The wings had to be entered through the main doorway in the front. The ranges had the doorways to the cells on the outside of the Building and one had to climb the Outside stairs to the landing in order to reach the cells there.

The two large "Wings", 3 and 4, were at the far end of the courtyard, then the OBS, then 5 Range and 6 Range. Yards 7, 8 and 9 were connected to the prison hospital.

My first stop after entering the main section was to line up, outside the kitchen block for something to eat, and was given a large dixie full of sliced up mutton, with some tomato gravy and half a loaf of oven-fresh bread. Carrying this then, I was led by the screw to a heavily padlocked Barrel Gate in between A Wing and Five Range, which led to the OBS. I was admitted into the OBS and given over to "Woody" (Mr Woodridge) a two striper, a man with a fat face and neck and thick hands and fingers, he had little squinted "pigs eyes" and had been the OBS officer for a long time from all I could gather.

Despite his somewhat repelling outward appearance "Woody" was not such a bad apple and would even help you if he could, he was pretty well liked by the OBS crims, who had anything to do with him.

"Harper" was his senior there and had the "dog" tag put upon him by the inmates, a three striper of somewhat unsavoury disposition in regard to "crims".

They gave me a cell with another guy we shall call Tommy Adams, a crim who I came to know for a lot of years afterward. Life in this OBS section was pretty confined, the exercise yard was only about 30 feet by about 40 feet, and had a "park chess-table" kind of a setup with seats and a roof over it, right in the centre.

In the yard, during the day, the inmates would keep busy by doing whatever the facilities at hand would allow. This could be just sitting and playing chess or cards, or walking or doing exercises or playing handball or anything like this. I met several guys up on murder "raps" and strangely enough they all seemed nice enough people, when you'd get down to walking, talking and so on.

Also a lot of weird characters and con-men like Murray Roberts, or Fat Tony the 'dago' who used to like to sing all night, if you could call it singing) just to keep everyone awake. 'The Jew', who had some kind of mental phobia maybe that had stayed with him since, the death camps or something but he used to walk back and forth in his cell and scream out "Eichmann! Eichmann!" at the top of his voice.

In the cells there, you would be locked up for an hour at lunch time. At night the lights were left on, right throughout (all night). You got used to it (sleeping with the lights on) after a while. The beds were nothing but a coir mat, with a couple of blankets – no pillow. The trip tubs were made of heavy rubber and hard to use. There were ordinary screws on duty; they must have taken it in shifts. Sometimes they had to use restraining methods and they had strait jackets and padded cells and various other methods of restraint etc.

I spent about two and a half months in the OBS awaiting my trial. At last the time came and I was called up to front the judge about midway through the month of April. I fronted up real cool and unnerved about the whole thing. I was advised to take the public defender Mr Vizzard QC for my legal aid, who said the best I could hope for would be a decision of GP – Governor's Pleasure. So I agreed to accept this approach. ('Governor's Pleasure' was basically a plea that the accused was insane at the time of the crime and that, as a result, he should be detained for as long as the Governor wished until there was evidence of a return to sanity, repentance and the possibility of release into society without any further danger. For many under 'Governor's Pleasure', it was a life sentence.)

The Judge agreed upon the GP after a brief consideration, and I was led back down into the lockup to await transportation back to the "Bay". They took me back to Long Bay along with a bunch of other guys, who had also just received their sentence. Most of these guys were doing time for "busts", break and enter, or "armed Rob" or things like this, so when they'd ask me, "What did you get yours for pal?" and I'd tell them, "I got mine for wasting my mum and dad with a sawn down shotgun". Well then their eyebrows would go up and I'd get response like, "Not bad! Not bad". But mostly they would say "Gees, Bob, what did you do that for, pal?" to which I would reply, "I dunno, things just finished up that way" or something to that effect.

When I got back to the Bay, I was given two new sets of 'Boob Uniform', blue denim jackets and trousers and two sets of flannel underwear, and two number tags which I had to have sown onto my jacket, just above the left side pocket, mine was 1332. They told me I was to be housed up in 1 Range and was told to report to the screw in charge.

Well I started off across the courtyard, towards 1 Range, and as I was going across the courtyard there I am aware that all these crims in the surrounding yards, have stopped whatever they are doing, and are somewhat curiously and apprehensively "pegging me off". Well now, I reach the 1 Range gate there, and am waiting for the screw there to admit me, which at last he does, and almost immediately upon entering I get a kind, cool reception, and I hear these guys in the yard murmuring to one another, "This is the guy Cox who did in his Ma and Pa with a sawn down shotgun". "Yeah! No kid!" And "Bullshit!" And "Fair Dinkum". But mostly, the looks I am getting from the majority of these pilgrims is one with a considerable amount of "respect" if you don't mind using that word.

But then, there are these certain three guys who don't look so impressed as the rest. This trio are an undividable clique and the "heavies" of the Range. So now, I will describe these three that stuck in my memory there that time of my admittance.

The middle guy is Bob (Bob Mabry) he is the leader with angular cheek bones, cold steely blue eyes that stare straight at you. His hair cut is a flat top crew-cut and he's about five foot eight and well built. Rod Davies, his right hand, smallish, like a jockey, with very dark hair and eyes. He wears his shirt buttoned all the way up. His hat has been salted (for stiffness) and he has creases in his trousers, where he has pressed them under his mattress, the night before. Now last, but by no means least is Morrie (the knuckle man of the three, Morrie

Gearin). He is a bit taller than Rod, though similarly built, his mouth is crooked, like with a perpetual sarcastic smile that goes with the deep blue-eyed stare, and every now and then he twitches his whole head and neck to one side. So these three come over and I get the pretty obvious impression that these three "heavy" characters are some kind of a self-appointed welcoming committee, but by the same token I make sure that I don't let on that I have taken too much notice of these three characters.

Well I get my cell card and towel and sheets and pillow slip and a cake of soap, like I am supposed to, and I make my way up the stairs to the landing where I am fixing my cell card into the frame outside my cell doorway, like I am supposed to do, when I am approached by these three guys. Bob speaks out. "Hey Bud!" he says.

"Yeah!" I reply.

"You're the new guy who has just got 'sloughed' for rubbing his parents aincha?" and I reply.

"Yeah! Pal that is me OK, so what is that to you Pal?" I speak like this because, at this time I am young, only nineteen years old, and not afraid of these three guys, because my good common sense has told me that in this joint, if I do not have as much bluff as the next guy and stick up for myself, well then I am going to be walked on and trodden into the ground. I know this will never happen because I do not intend to let it.

Well Bob begins to speak again, and the three kind of hustle all around me till I am forced to step into my cell doorway, then he continues, "I like you Bob" (speaking to me) and brushing an imaginary hair strand off my jacket. "Yeah? No kid?" I am starting to wonder what is coming next, when he continues.

"Yeah – well it's like this, Bob. Us three run this wing see!"

"Somebody has to be on top in a joint like this, so in this wing we are it see, but don't get the idea that we lean on the little guys. Gees! We would never do that, no sir, we help any guy we can, and if we see any big guys trying to hustle smaller guys or anything like that, well we step in and break it up. You get the idea don't you, Bob?" So I said.

"Yeah Pal, I suppose I do", and I start to think that maybe this crew might do more good than harm at that. Anyway I am not a goddamn crusader for truth honour and the American way, so I say back to Bob the leader, "Yeah! OK buddies, so you three are the top guys in the wing here so what has that got to do with me?" and I am told.

"No! It's OK but we know that after what you done, you are a willing kind of guy, so we just want to check to make sure we have you for a friend and not an enemy, you get the drift?" So then I say again.

"No Pal, I couldn't care less!" So after that, we all shake hands all round and finish up real good friends.

Well then I spend a couple of days there like this getting to feel the joint out, so to speak and basically I find out that the majority of these crims in here are guys with a chip on their shoulder towards the outside society – reform school dropouts – if you like, who make crime of some kind their paying lifestyle. They figure it like this, the world is like this, one big con – everybody (even reputably) honest and upstanding citizens like politicians and police, and even ministers of God for that matter, are trying to con everybody, and everybody is trying to con everybody else and rip each other off and 'bullshitting' in each other's earhole about every 'frigging thing'. So these guys think, "What the hell, first in best dressed. I'll get in and do my own share of ripping. Man's law is all a lot of bullshit and corruption, so I'll use the good common sense and the two hands that God has given me and if any bastard gets in the road, well God help them". So this is the basic attitude of these guys who I begin to rub shoulders with, and I must admit here, right here and now, that there is a whole lot to be said for their point of view. Like somebody once said, "If it wasn't for the fear of the reprisals, well everybody would be rebelling against the system".

So like I said before, I start to rub shoulders and make friends with these guys, There are Bust Experts (Break and Enter), Armed Rob guys, also smash and grab men, even an occasional tank man (Safe Breaker) and of course, Shop Lifters (some more expertise than others). Some would just never stop, and wouldn't if given the opportunity.

We spend all our spare time then playing poker, for weed (tobacco), and doing a lot of joking, bragging and 'bullshitting' to each other about who is who in the underworld and who has copped what lagging – and for what, and all this kind of crim jargon and malarkey. But usually the truthful guys who know what they are talking about and who are speaking from experience, are easily detectable from the 'bullshitters' and braggarts.

On the weekdays then, in the "can" you had to go. to work just like outside people, if you didn't, well you wouldn't get paid, and consequently you wouldn't get a buy-up – which inmates are allowed once a week.

So everybody goes to their allotted jobs in the different workshops and there is plenty of work in these days of my internment – such as the Mat Shop where you are taught how to weave coir mats, the Brick Shop where they make bricks and stack them and deliver them to different work gangs throughout the prison. Then there is of course, the builders, the plumbers, electricians, and more "cushy" jobs such as office workers, typists and "tea boys" and librarians etc. – and other indispensable jobs such as the cooks, the bakers and hospital attendants and so forth and so on. Lots of crims are qualified in various types of trade and most are adapt and useful in one way or another. Very few crims like to be "malingerers". Nearly all prefer to make themselves useful in some way.

Jobs like the kitchen hands and cooks, and the bakers in gaol are particularly good jobs, and the fringe benefits are plentiful, but of course at this time I am new and unaware of these facts, so I am detailed to work along with several other guys from 1 Range where I live.

We are detailed to work in Shop No 4, where they sent out nuts and bolts and washers and various other pieces of stuff of this nature, and count them and wrap them up in tar paper and stick them up with tape into bundles and stack the bundles into assorted lots to await dispensation somewhere.

So this 4 Shop is a real weird kind of place as it turns out, and I am hearing all this immoral kind of talk and guys talking about homosexuality and various other things of an extremely common and immoral nature. Well this particular day, I went into the toilet for a smoke like very many of the guys would do all the time. So this time I went in and there is a great lot of laughing and all this kind of business going on. They had this new young guy that had only just started in the Shop. They had made this kid strip down to his bare skin. He was as naked as a jaybird and all tied up from head to foot with 3/4" sticky scotch tape and blindfolded and they were using this guy to play "put a tale on the donkey". I couldn't work out whether the "donkey guy" was enjoying the game or not.

Food

The food that the regular crim was given at this particular period of time in Long Bay left a lot to be desired to say the least. Nine times out of ten the meat would be boiled mutton, with a various array of side lashings such as a bit of boiled cabbage or spinach or mashed potato or pumpkin or sometimes some rather tasteless coleslaw in the summertime. Or the alternative would be "grey death" stew which would be nearly as bad as its name depicts (more gravy than meat). We were told that these "main courses" were more than enough to keep us felons adequately nourished. Bulldust! I would like to see the governor or the screws eat that rubbish that we were given.

During those years of my internment I had about five eggs in about six or seven years. Two from a cook at Goulburn, and another three later when I went to Parramatta, but during these times, the ordinary crim never saw an egg. The best and most nourishing meal would probably be the ground oatmeal porridge that we were given in a dixie for breakfast, this with a ration of sugar daily and a ration of milk together with half a loaf of freshly baked bread daily and a carton of treacle or jam which was issued weekly. These things would usually be sufficient to see that most crims could do their lagging out without starving to death. On Sundays we would get Plum Duff and custard. Amenities were four ounces of tobacco and matches and cigarette papers. Weekend movies and sports were also categorised as amenities.

In order to go to the movies at the weekend, every inmate in the various exercise yards would file past the screw that was assigned to check that particular yard, usually a 3-striper, with probably a crown or a crown and stripe looking on, and these would check you for clean clothes and appearance, polished shoes (big cans of "nugget" boot polish and brushes and rags were always supplied to the yards at the weekend), tied up shoelaces, buttons all done up, "OK. You're right, number so and so". But if you didn't have everything up to A1 scratch, like maybe a button undone, or an untied shoelace, or something like this, then you would find yourself back in the exercise yard for the whole afternoon. Every crim was also expected to be clean shaven on these days.

The laundry was an extremely important and mostly efficient part of prison activity and provided several varied jobs. The laundry would wash everybody's clothes and underwear but we had to wash our own woollen socks. In later years, they gave us nylon socks that were a lot easier.

The discipline in the jails in these days was as you might expect. Strict, that just about sums it up. They marched you in line to and from work and the same as with the movies if you came on a work muster with a button undone, or an untied shoelace, well you could very easily cop a back-hander that would bring tears of hate to your eyes, and make you bite your lip to hold back the curses.

Bob, Rod and Morrie had a pretty neatly organised bit of contraband, smuggling and dealing going on for themselves, and me, in the various parts of the prison where it counted, and there was always some joker coming over to the bars of the yard and after checking to make sure that the coast was clear, would shove some big bundle through to the receiver, who would take it down the yard and share it out. Usually there would be maybe a half a side of baked lamb all cut up into pieces, or two or three whole plum duffs all sliced up or even loaves of buttered bread, or anything else they could lay their hands on. Fresh tomatoes and onions were also quite acceptable when obtainable.

Of course these guys weren't obtaining these "goodies" for nought, nobody takes risks in gaol (or anywhere else) for that matter for nothing, and favours like this had to have adequate payment. In the 'boob', they call this kind of dealing "working hot" and nearly everybody does their share of "working hot" at one time or another. The screws know that it goes on, but mostly, they are not really worried, and unless they get special orders in some given direction – well, they prefer to let it go. Of course you get these new guys, "rookies", screws who have just started on the job and are anxious to show how conscientious they are. – Now for a while these guys (some are worse than others), give everyone concerned one big headache with that over expedient zeal in efficient work. They have to be reporting everybody and writing everybody's number down in their little books, till at last the governor has to say to the person, "Look, officer so and so, ease off. Bend with the breeze a bit in regard to the men. They are men you know, not school kids and we don't want a riot on our hands".

Now these dumb perfectionists would get very "browned off" about being reprimanded when all they were trying to do was to do their job to the best of their ability (And in consequence they would quit the job). "Good bloody riddance too, the poor dumb bastards just couldn't understand it at all".

Not too long after this, I was classified for a prison suite for long serving prisoners. The logical choice was Goulburn, so one foggy morning I find myself with my number patches torn off and clambering aboard the escort bus, bound for Goulburn Gaol, along with Rod, Morrie and some others.

Goulburn Gaol

We are handcuffed together in pairs and cannot see out of the opaque glass windows, just through the front windscreen. So it is no wonder that we are all glad when we finally reach our destination and get off the bus. So we get off and are looking at this Goulburn Prison. Our first impressions of the place are not all that good. The prison is situated right on the top of high ground, overlooking the town but the thing that is most noticeable about it is the freezing cold wind. So we are all standing there huddling up and waiting for the screw to check us off the list, which he pretty soon does. So then we are led through the front section of the prison near to the Prison Hospital. It has a nice front lawn and some flower gardens – a bit more picturesque than the "Bay". The Prison Chapel is plainly visible from where we are and I am looking at the brightly painted windows, when some other crim tells me that Lennie Lawson did the artwork there.

I had heard of Len Lawson. His name used to appear on the front cover of two of Australia's best known monthly western comic books – *The Lone Avenger* and *The Hooded*

Riders. There were usually pretty-faced, busty young girls shown in these comics, but nothing out of the ordinary. So it to most people's surprise when Lennie was charged with raping some five young models after bailing them up and taking them to deserted spot in French's Forest. He got a life sentence for that. Raping five young models, maybe he figured it was worth a life sentence.

So we go through into the main courtyard which is a half circle surrounded by the four – cell blocks (wings), each of these is three tiers high. The hub section (the section directly opposite the four wings) is divided into the shower room and storeroom (downstairs) and the Library, Chapel and Movie Theatre (upstairs). There is a high wall which surrounds the prison and various work buildings of various nature, workshops and places of daily occupation all around the perimeter.

They give us all our lunch and lock us all together in a double cell where we can have a rest and talk a bit and enjoy our lunch. We took the lid off our dixie. It was a really nice thick curried stew, a hotpot full of diced up vegetables and corned meat and a half a loaf of nice oven fresh bread.

It tasted so good, and I can feel the strength and energy coming back into my eyeballs as I eat. I must have been half starved and so must we all. I manage to comment on the tucker, how good it tastes, to Rod and Morrie and they manage a grunt, but mostly they are too busy wolfing it down. Like I said, we were all half starved for decent food.

After I have eaten my meal and my eyeballs are feeling the benefit on behalf of my whole body, I start thinking to myself. '*Well if this is my first glimpse of Goulburn Gaol, it is not too bad after all*'.

So we are all issued with new "clobber" similar to the Bay but with an extra set of cold weather blue woollen gear, something like the air force guys wear, and woollen "long John" underwear, and woollen socks and a belt and hat etc. (We were issued with boots and shoes when we needed them) I suppose we must have looked pretty funny to outsiders dressed there like that. There were undoubtedly a lot of things about Goulburn that made it easier for a guy like myself, doing a long stretch. But don't get the idea that the discipline here at Goulburn was in anyway slack. No sir, it was just a severe as anywhere else and if you failed to toe the line or wanted to make trouble, well you would still receive the same old back hander, or the same old whack with the baton, if they figured that you deserved it.

Heavy biffs were usually reserved for special inmates who wanted to "have a go" or to "carry on a bit" and were usually delivered by a three striper to supervise, a two striper to lead (through experience) and two or three rookies to assist. If this kind of chastisement was not enough to discourage the person in question, well he would likely as not find himself on his way to some other place where they would be given "notice" and ready to give this person a warm reception when the 'poor bastard' arrived.

Places like Bathurst and the notorious Grafton (the "Expertee Centre" for coping with intractable prisoners) were usually the places kept for such operations. I had met tough guys! No, really tough crims, guys who were not satisfied till they had been to Grafton and tasted the medicine for themselves, but from all accounts they were not too talkative and did not seem anxious to let on just how bad the ordeal of Grafton Gaol had been for them.

Sometimes guys will test you to see if you will fight. Mostly if you find a guy like this, well it is better to fight the bloke there and then and get it over with, or the 'son of a bitch' will keep hounding you till you do. So all I can say is – fight the bloke, and give him one in the teeth, and then the 'wretched pissant of a b…' will probably shut his (unmentionable) mouth – or at least when he has seen that you are ready to have a go, well, you might swap a few punches and leave it at that.

If you do not stand up for your rights in the boob, well you will probably lose all self-respect and personal dignity and if that happens, well "God only knows" what is in store. Of course, these fighting challenges don't happen very often. In all of my fourteen and a half years as a crim, the event only cropped up two or three times, so you could probably say that in most cases, the average crim is satisfied to live day by day as peacefully as possible.

Of course then you may find a case of a guy who may be a staunch Christian and prefers to turn the other cheek, no matter what happens. When a case like this comes to hand, well the aggressor would very likely give up. I should think, a conscientious Christian is an immovable rock and I don't think that anybody would want to try kicking anyone like that, or even raising their hand against them.

I met some pretty weird crims there in A Yard, which was the yard that I was allotted to for most of the time (including weekends). Little Graham, called "Grib", was a feminine kind of little guy, but very polite to everybody and very friendly and quite intelligent. I heard some time later that "Grib" died (I'm not sure of what) but he was one nice little person I will always remember. Then there was Sammy, we shall call him

Sammy Crighton. I have changed the surnames a bit (to protect the innocent). Sammy was a hood. He came from Newtown and carried a rod or so he reckoned, an ex-World War Two US Army 45 Colt Automatic, which he carried in a shoulder holster under his right armpit as he pussyfooted around Newtown. He also had the nickname the "Newtown Shadow" or even the "man with a thousand heads", this last one was because of his acute case of acne.

There was Stephen Leslie Bradley who was charged and sentenced to Life for the Grahame Thorn kidnapping. He died at Goulburn later on from a heart attack I think. Then there was Billy Hayden, Reg Chakute and Michael Farruge who were usually hobnobbing it around King's Cross and who knew just about everybody who could be regarded as 'locals' of the Cross. They even knew or (knew about) guys like Lennie McPherson and Abe Saffron and who were the real heavies and there were guys who were just – "would be's if they could be's". There were those who were the best tank men, and con-men, and knew who was screwing who's girlfriend while they were in the "nick", and so forth and so on. The whole thing there, listening to guys like this, was "highly informative" and "very educational".

In gaol, there is supposed to be no money and neither is there, except if somebody happens to smuggle a 10, or 20, or even a 50 dollar note in, as they do sometimes.

But most of the dealing (as I have said before) is done in tobacco and if you have enough of it, you can buy lots of good things such as anything from a T-Bone steak and eggs meal, down to a hand knitted sweater or a homemade cosset or extra brand new blankets (if you need them) or even a brand new pair of spit-polished ox-blood shoes that shine like glass.

Some guys probably set out to spit polish their own brand new shoes or boots, and then, when they see what a fantastically good job they have done on them, well they decide to auction them off, and might come out with 20 to 30 ounces of weed for their trouble. Some handy guys used to make cigarette holders, colourful ones, out of pieces of cut up toothbrush handles, welded together with pieces of aluminium dixie lids – real ingenious people, crims. Never underestimate the mental power of a criminal.

Of course in this jungle, where honour has its own meaning to everybody in a diffcrent way, well you might find some "smart Alec" who will do a deal with you for something or other, and then decide then he is too tough or smart, so he decides he will refuse to pay up – this is called "brassing", and a guy who gets the reputation of being a Brasser is a guy who pretty soon loses any friends that he might previously have had. With crims, a deal is a deal, and meant to be honoured, if you try to brass somebody, the word gets around and you might find yourself pretty soon seeking attention in the Prison Hospital, for anything ranging from a blackened eye or a few lose teeth – to even a well-placed "shiv" (knife) in between your ribs.

As most people can appreciate, no one likes to be made a fool of, but some people just never seem to learn. If they do, it's the hard way.

The Tailor's Shop

So they gave me my first full time job, and I was allotted to work in the Tailor's Shop. The Tailor's Shop then (later they built a new one) was located up above the Carpenters, over on the left side wall of the Prison. We used to have to ascend to the outside landing there (which ran along the full length of the building) by two sets of steel staircases, which ran up from the ground onto the landing. Inside there was some long benches, on which were set, side by side, a number of old post-war electric Singers machines, on which the more experienced machinists were allowed to work.

Then there were the old pedal machines situated around the sides near the walls where people who just started would be put till they got the idea of making clothes etc.

They would be given a bundle of denims, or shirt pieces or whatever, which were all cut up, according to their various patterns by the cutter, who had his bench downstairs. If you could handle the pedal machine with a reasonable amount of prowess, well then, they would put you on an electric machine.

There were other jobs there too, such as the presser. They had two steam presses and an ironer, for ironing small articles, and the store man, whose job it was to put everything away when the articles were completed – the storeman was also expected to give out the bundles of unmade garments and to keep a ledger on everything that was given out and handed in (completed).

There were also jobs as broom boys or sweepers – these jobs were usually given to new beginners for a while, and then they would be given something more dignified to work at when a vacancy occurred.

Mr Hans the German was in charge of the old Tailor's Shop when I first went there to work. Some guys there seemed to hate him, by the way that they spoke, maybe it was just because he was a German. There are always people who will be resentful and like to be nasty especially to foreigners.

Personally I always found him a fair and quietly spoken man, except when someone would cheek him or stir him up. The German seemed to like me for some reason, but he was also careful to show no favouritism to anyone. I liked the German. If circumstances had been different, I reckon we might have been good friends. I never saw him write his name so maybe this "Mr Hans" or just "Hans" may have been just some kind of nickname given to him by the crims – to others he was just "The German".

Well as it all happened, the German was the only one screw in charge of the tailor's shop – as he had been for some time, from all I could gather. Well, his loneliness in this job pretty soon came to an end, with the arrival of Matthews, a screw who was put on as his assistant. Matthews was a middle aged old guy with a beakish nose and dark eyes, and hair and moustache. He called me "Hughie" and was friendly and helpful to everyone in his manner. (Bob earned the nick-name 'Baby Hughie' because of his big girth. It reminded many of the comic book character, the giant 'Baby Hughie'.) Matthews seemed very efficient in his job, and seemed to know all about tailoring that was quite obvious right from the start.

Also I got the idea from his outward appearance, his surname, and the fact that he seemed to know the tailoring business back to front – well I got this strong impression that he may well have been Jewish, either in religion or more likely just by blood or possibly both.

Anyway from the time that Matthews arrived on the scene, it seemed notably evident that he and the "German" were going to be at "logger heads". One day after he (Matthews) had been arguing with the German about some detail or other, it was much to all of us watching great amusement that the German whipped off his jacket, and was all about declaring Matthews on in a bout of fisticuffs. The poor old German must have had as much of it as he could take – because one day he just didn't show up for work anymore.

There were two guys in the Tailor's Shop by the name of "Johnna", Johnson. There was Johnna who had a decent sized nose and claimed to be a Jew. He also played the cornet a bit.

Then there was the other Johnna, a nice young guy, with a bit of a mug lair streak, which maybe he had got from his old man, who used to be a Fitzroy trigger man and who had been shot dead by the police, maybe back in the days of Squizzy Tailor or something like this.

Then there was Tom, on the iron who wasted some guy he didn't like, Phil Solway. Morrie Gearin was also there in the Tailor's. There was Phil Makin who was doing life (a quiet scholarly schoolboy type). He worked on the twin needle machine for doing the seams. There were others. Johnny Rankmore – life. Young Ritchie, blond and blue eyes like the depths of the ocean. Bob Cherry, blond hair, blue eyes and camp, but not to be stirred about his sexual preferences – he could and would "go off" if necessary. And then there was "Eugene" who used to work on the broom and was as "camp as Chloe" and talked funny – he couldn't help it he was a pussy cat.

Then there were Thommo, and Lennie Splite, partners in crime and inseparable buddies. Bob Skidmore, Lennie Hastel, whose brother Ray tore all of his clothes off in the courtroom and raced up, stark naked and tried to punch the judge on the nose before they eventually restrained him. Then there was Carl Snierdahl and Paddy O'Niel, who I knew for years after, and last but by no means least "Al" Alex Heyden, as skinny as a broom handle. Al was one special character.

Matthews was tireless in his efforts and productivity whereas Mr Hans had been satisfied to go on just "getting along" and running the place as it had been for years previously. Matthews, on the other hand, was a bottomless well of ideas always coming up with some new improvement or other – and it wasn't for nothing. Pretty soon the authorities began to pay heed to Matthews and soon with the help of Wally McGeaghan who was Controller – General of Prisons at the time – well the news soon got around that Matthews had got the go ahead to build a brand new two story tailors shop and equip it from top to bottom with all brand new equipment and machinery.

They placed a couple of screws in charge upstairs and a couple downstairs and after that we all wondered what happened to Matt. Sooner or later then we got a glimpse of him, but only briefly. He was tearing around the place but not in his old screw's attire. No sir, now he was all dressed up in a navy-blue pinstriped double breasted suit with a blue silk shirt and tie and a black felt hat. I was highly impressed with Matthews.

So like I stated previously, Matt was a nice guy and if you knew him, you could hardly help liking him, and I got the feeling that basically it was probably a damn good thing for most of us, when he came. But still, I used to like Mr Hans and I often wondered what became of him as well.

I knew Wally McGeaghan well even to talk to. We were on a first name acquaintanceship me and Wally – would you believe that? Yes it's true and when he would come up the stairs in the Tailor's Shop he would say, "How's it going, Hughie?" to which I would reply rather impertinently I suppose. "Good, Wal" or "Great Guns, Wally How are you?" Like I have stated Wally was one real nice guy – too nice probably, that's why I suppose that· they gave him "the big A" (the "Arse" – they sacked him) at some time later.

The Governor then was K, a stern "son of a bitch" to say the least – the less we say about him the better for everybody. Then after him came Jack, Jack H, or "chatty Jack" to the crims. He wasn't a bad old mongrel, whose bark was always a lot worse than his bite – a guy with a sense of humour at least. He was given the "chatty" tag because of his somewhat sloppy way of dressing.

Then the last governor of Goulburn while I was there was T, a very strict conservative, a grey flannel suit guy, who kept his position. I never had any face to face dealings with T, so maybe he was OK, I don't know but I will give him the benefit of the doubt.

Like as you the reader can get the gist by these Governors I have told you about who came and went – I spent a lot of cold winters at Goulburn Gaol, but maybe it wasn't all that bad – it was a life of its own and you would have to experience it to know just what I mean. All I can say is, I knew some old lags who had done close to thirty years inside, and do you know what? They didn't want to go out, and if the parole board talked about giving them a go outside – they would tell them – "Forget it, I am staying right where I am".

Well like I said before, there were these cold Goulburn winters. The wind there would blow right through to your bones, up on that hill, and there was no interior heating just blankets, closed doors, warm clothing, and plenty of hot food, exercise and sensibly stimulating conversation among your fellow inmates.

Sensibly stimulating conversation was not hard to find there. There were guys all the time who would be only too pleased to talk to you about anything you liked, be it current affairs or politics or bionic genetics or the future of mankind or even theology or whatever. There was a good prison library and lots of the more "scholarly types" would spend all their spare time soaking up knowledge.

We looked forward to the weekends with some eagerness because it meant the distribution of weekly buy ups (where you could also purchase "grouse" (good quality tobacco and even a pipe if you were a pipe smoker). Besides there was the other food and drink items. Also the weekends meant sports and movies. There were always these very involved card games in the yard for weed and some of the guys would have their own bags of poker or pontoon "chips" made out of pieces of thick leather and stamped with the significant number – they (the games) were all very "legit". Hand ball was always popular in the yards, or just walking, talking or pacing back and forth.

Well as you know by what I have previously stated, my years in Goulburn went all the way back to the German and the old Tailor Shop – now there were only a few of us long timers who could lay claim to that, and while we were here in the new Tailor's, we saw an almost endless line of new young guys come and go.

The Captain

It was about this time that "the captain" came. "The captain" was one hell of character and made a pretty good hit among the crims right from the beginning. He was the kind of guy that one might very well meet, once in a whole lifetime and whenever you would see him. Johnny Farrer was his real name. He would be in the yard – surrounded by other guys just listening to him talk. He could tell great stories or maybe take some poor guy who nobody would talk to and put him on a pedestal and talk about him to the other guys in the yard. Not to ridicule him, just to try and make this poor "nobody of a guy" feel good and before long he would have this poor guy laughing and feeling real happy and everybody else would be laughing and give John a good long clap for his effort.

Well to get on with the story, John was a great gambler, be it poker, or horseraces or a cockroach race or you name it – well then, you can bet Johnny would be there giving odds and would have a lot of guys interested and on Melbourne Cup days he would always run a couple of good sized sweeps.

If you saw him on the weekend, he would always be up to the ultimate "scratch" of the prison "best dressed element". Anybody could be among these best dressed, it would be up to the individual, on how much effort he desired to put into his appearance. As for my personal self, I was always physically clean and shaved and had my shoes always polished to the point of necessity and wore clean clothes.

But I don't think I ever ranked as a "boob" fashion plate, the same as some of these guys who went to extreme trouble. Maybe I should have been more like that. I suppose I will have to say I was too lazy to put in the required effort. They certainly stood out and made a good impression among the other crims, these guys, and there was also a lot of good natured rivalry, to see who could look just a little bit more "dapper" than the next guy.

Well anyway, John dressed very good like I have said, but when you saw him through the week-on-the work muster he would be dead beat from working there on the wood pile. I had worked on the wood pile when I started at Goulburn, but only for a short time, so I know just how hard the work was there. They really made you earn your porridge there on that job.

So after a while they gave John a better job for his trouble and put him to work up in the tailors shop as a sweeper, and for a long time he would keep us all amused while we were working by walking around and sweeping and cracking a joke here and there while he worked. He made this pair of epaulettes with stripes on them and pinned them onto the shoulders of his work jacket (just for a dig at the screws) to try and get them to bite (which they never did! They preferred to treat it a joke). So this is how Johnny got the nickname "the captain".

"Batman"

So, one day this new fellow came and they put him on the broom to work as John's assistant. We started to try to talk to this new guy to get him to settle down and "open up" a bit, but he just held on to this constant appearance of fretting and wouldn't even open up and talk about his problems. This was a great shame.

Now a guy like this who has problems, or who is doing high lagging pretty hard can be likened (if you like) to a pressure cooker. If he does not "open up" and discuss his problems to the other crims and let off a bit of steam here and there, well! His sanity is at stake.

You can guess, as well as the next person, that pretty soon, something must "give" somewhere. When it does, the result is not pretty to behold.

I think Johnny tried to the best of his ability to have this guy "open up" a bit. For the most part we could all see that his efforts were in vain.

Anyway, this nice bright sunny day, I am standing at the upstairs window, looking out, across the prison wall onto the meadows and river. Turning around for a brief moment, I notice this new fellow put his broom very meticulously up against the wall and start off downstairs. I didn't take too much notice of this and resumed looking out of the window.

Just a short way away from the Tailor's Shop, and easily visible from my window, is the roof of the boiler house, next door to which there leads a steel staircase from the ground. All of a sudden, this new 'cove' appears on the roof, and I can see right away that he has something on his mind.

He walks up to the edge of the boiler house (poor so-and-so) and makes some crazy haywire mental calculations in his brain. He then proceeds to shed his jacket and go back to obtain as much of a run as he can muster. (I still couldn't believe that he was actually going to try to leap from the boiler house onto the prison wall! It must have been a potential leap of about 12 feet and the prison wall would have been at least about 14 feet higher.) Sure enough, away he goes, and he launches himself into space like some super-hero or something! (No wonder the crims gave him the nickname 'Batman'.)

Well Batman hits the wall about halfway down. (I suppose the jump he made was pretty good, all things considered.)

I can see also that the poor cove is in a bad way and I start to think that, at this time, maybe his earthly worries are over for good. But No! Crims start running from all directions and for a while, nobody touches the poor blighter.

But then, after a while, some guy comes along from the Carpenter's Shop with a wheelbarrow and they bundle this poor guy intro it, with his legs hanging over the side, and they wheel him away to the hospital. From there, I heard later, that his condition was "satisfactory".

"The Winger"

They let this other new fellow into our yard (God only knows why) and he is making everybody feel 'blasted well' ill at ease with his perpetual winging. The ratbag was only doing a couple of weeks gaol! He must have been a few cents short! Every time you would look, he would be bending somebody's ear about this and that. He couldn't wait to get out – and all this. At last, Johnny S stood up one day and said, "I'm going to kill him" We all laughed a bit, but by the expression on Johnny's face, we could see that he really meant it. He would have killed this guy if we hadn't restrained him. But after a while we managed to calm him down.

So this night, it is summer and most of the gaol is pretty restless and there is a lot of 'yelling out' going on.

I have a cell on the top landing, and you don't have to guess too long or hard to figure who I have in the cell in front of me, –yes, the "Winger". Well, I was lying there and listening to the various bits of 'calling out' going on all around. Pretty soon, this screw, an Irishman, and not a bad kind of fellow, (and I knew him a bit), yells out, as he had done already a couple of times, – "Hey, you men up there! Keep the noise down, or I'll come up and quieten you!" So, feeling a bit cheeky this night, I am up to the window bars and singing out back down to him various insults.

(Forgive the language. That's how I was at that time.)

"Hennessey!" (Not his real name.) "You Irish Mick retard! You couldn't heat manure – with a shovel, you (flipping) Irish manure-head!"

Then there was a short pause till he realises what was being said and he cries out, "Who was it that said that?"

Then I yelled back, "I did, you Irish bloody poofter bastard! What are you going to do about it?"

Now at this, everybody starts to laugh and cheer. Then, I could tell by the hurried sounds of locks on the Wing doors being unlocked and chains being rustled, that Hennessey is now in none too savoury a mood. He has to climb to the top landing and I can hear his footsteps coming from a long way off. By the time he makes it to the top and starts down along my side of the landing, well poor old Hennessey is puffing and wheezing like Stephenson's Rocket.

He stops outside my cell to catch his breath. (Thus, I calculate. Not a bad guess, I think.) Then he unlocks the lock on my door and comes into the cell. (I am pretending to be sound asleep by now and have my light out.) He says.

"Baby Hughie, was that you talking back to me from up here?"

I said, "No, Sir, Mr Hennessey. It is that Smart-Alec bastard in the next cell in front of me. He's been talking all day and winging about how Irish Catholics are the dumbest bastards on God's earth". I could almost see the expression on Hennessey's face.

"Did he now?" he said and slammed my door on his way out.

Next minute the next door cell is opened and…

Belt! Belt! Belt! Flog! Flog! This to the screams of, "Help! Jesus! (Manure!)" and "Bloody Hell! What's this for?" and Hennessey's voice. "Stupid Catholics is it? Well. This will hold you for a while!" Then there were a few more screams and flogs.

The next morning, we lined up for breakfast and I was quite satisfied to see this winging so-and-so nursing a couple of fair sized bruised lumps on the side of his head and jaw.

Now he had something real to be a winger about….

Everybody thought it was a real distribution of justice, especially Johnny S.!

The Bulgarian

Another John, Johnny B. was a Bulgarian, and we were good friends. He had a grey, close-cropped haircut and a kind of tubby figure. We would spend a lot of time walking and talking. Johnny had everybody all figured out.

Sometimes, if he saw someone sitting and brooding a bit – as I did sometimes – (I didn't always feel in a good mood) – he would approach them, or me.

"Hey, Hughie. Come on. Let's walk. I got a lot of things to tell you". To which, after a while, I would get up and we would start to talk while pacing, back and forth.

Then he'd tell me: "See that fellow. He is as mad as a hatter. He did this, and he said that, and to top it all he beats up on his wife!" I would say "Fair Dinkum, Johnny! How do you know all this, mate?" He would say to me, "You! You're young, you whippersnapper". Then, "I just knows, that's all".

He certainly was in the know, but secretly, I knew how he knew so much about all these other crims. He would walk and talk with these guys and then, ever so casually, he would wrangle this information out of them when they were not really on their guard about the questions he might ask.

He was as cunning as a latrine-house rat. When he would start to try this questionnaire business with me, I would just turn around and look straight into his face and start to laugh. To this, he would act like he was ever so hurt and that I had really wounded his feelings.

He would say, "All right! If you don't want to talk!" and pretend to walk away.

But he really wasn't too bad and he knew I was awake to his little tricks. That is why he told me about himself. He had received that same sentence ("Governor's pleasure") as I had received. He had killed his wife and the fellow whom he had caught with her in her infidelity to him. He had caught them in bed together and he had gone straight through the bedroom window with a carving knife in his hand. It was the thought of her deceit that sent him into a blind rage that could only be satisfied by blood. This he explained to me and he felt sure that God would understand too about these things.

I said, "Sure, Johnny. God understands everyone" That made him feel somewhat better, I could tell.

He told me that he owned a couple of flats down near William Street, King's Cross, Sydney, somewhere.

He told me of all the funny tenants he had in these flats. There was a Jewish family who used to invite him in sometimes to share their special "Prayers to God" feast day. He told me of the beautiful young daughters they had and all the nice Jewish food they shared, and so on.

He also told me about his girlfriend Maria Z. (Yes, alas, he killed his wife for infidelity, but he was none too faithful himself!) He said that Maria was always doing her best to seduce him.

"She was very pretty", he told me, and she had lovely big tits with nice big nipples. "She never wore a bra. She didn't need one but let her breasts sway seductively". He (Johnny) would go to fix her sink or do some other renovation or something that she had dreamed up, and before he knew what was going on, she had poured a couple of drinks into him and would be trying to take his clothes off. "She also used to make very nice 'sashleeke' or souse", he told me. This was some sort of European dish made from the meat of pickled pig's head with a lot of garlic, and it was left till it set like a jelly. This would be served with black olives, Greek feta cheese, German black pumpernickel bread and plenty of good Aussie Beer. "Ah, that's the way to live!" Johnny would say. "Forget about the women, Bobbie. They will only give you more troubles than you deserve".

He also told me about the Germans. Most Germans he had known were good, sincere, and, in most cases, very religious people who were very friendly.

"Then, on the other hand, the Russkies (Russians) were made, crazy bastards, capable of anything", he told me. "But the Russian women were very nice and sexy. But never trust a Russian". That was his advice to me and I supposed that he must have been talking truly, having known both.

The "Riot at Goulburn"
(Such as it was.)

The Prisons in New South Wales had all begun to "go out" in strikes for this and that and basically for the prison system to be "looked into" by the authorities, and for changes to be made in the way of rules and regulations that would make the place a better, more humane environment for people (crims) to live under.

We had heard it all on the news that Maitland and Long Bay and Parramatta had all put up their different "shows", usually with a minimum amount of violence, from what I could gather. – So now, we started to figure, "Well, now it" our turn.

Anyway, one thing did seem to grow more and more evident, and that was that there would have to be some drastic improvements made to the current system.

So it was this hot afternoon in the middle of summer, and probably about November of '69, but that is only a guess. I never made a note of the actual date.

We had all just "knocked off" work for the day.

All the Gaols had "gone out" except us and Bathurst. (They were saving theirs as something real special.) So the word was passed around, that today we were going to stay out, in protest. Well now, there were some who didn't like the idea, but they weren't a majority, so in the finish, we all agreed, more or less. This was except for the cowards, who slunk into their cells, when they thought no-one had been watching. They do not share in the honour of those who were willing to stand up for the rights of people in these circumstances. We will forget them.

Even "Bubbles" stayed out with us. He was a real nice, likeable, fat and pudgy fellow. He was a bit effeminate and had a bit of a lisp and big blue eyes. The guys all liked Bubbles. He was a 'sticker', a 'staunchie' and a real "digger" we will give him all the credit that is his due.

So at the time when everyone sat down in the yard and refused to move, (a 'sit-down' – the "Goulburn Riot") well Bubbles was there, right along with all the rest, the poor guy, his face and his big round eyes were an expression of absolute terror; but he wouldn't allow himself to weaken.

That day the voice came through the PA (Public Address) system to fall in as we were used to doing on the yellow muster line for tea, but this time nobody moved. So they started to repeat the order, over and over again – each time becoming more and more indignant than the one previous. They tried to hide their indignation, by coming on with this "buttering up" approach, and telling us how they would be willing to forget the whole incident, and how we had been given a "fair go" and all this bloody "crap" (as we thought) till we felt we were going to be "suffocated with manure" and throw up. "Horsedung! Who did these pissant bs think they were talking to?" Maybe they thought we were a bunch of kindergarten kids or something. Well no "b" was going to move and no "b" did! We didn't give an inch.

But I could see from the facial expression on Bubble's face that all of this tension was taking its toll on him, as time was slowly and gradually ticking past. The screws didn't like it at all, they took off their caps and jackets and ties and their resentment was very evident. They started muttering to each other, and had scowls on their faces like underfed dogs. Their sleeves were rolled up over their elbows and they had their night sticks and batons in their hands brandishing them at us in a threatening manner.

The Governor came down to confront us with his share of "bulldust". But we weren't in the mood "to be bullmanured to" – for our money and from where we stood, he could take his grey flannel suit and shove it right where it deserved to be shoved.

So we had these two guys with a bit of guts, Max and Doc who had agreed to act as spokesmen on behalf of the other crims. Max was a short little guy who had done a fair share of "boob", about 55 years old or thereabouts. The other guy Doc was much younger, only in his twenties and worked in the Hospital. They had this list of grievances written down and they walked down to the gate and presented this list to the governor, who promised us that he would read it, at the same time trying to talk us into going back inside.

Bubbles had a kind of fit, poor guy. He couldn't hack it anymore; he lay down on his side in the yard and began to have palpitations, with the tears streaming down his face. So they agreed to let two of the crims in the yard carry him inside to his cell, where he could rest.

Now we didn't know if at any moment these screws were, or were – not-going to get the word from the Governor, to come into the yard where we were, and start to bash us with their batons. They were obviously prepared and waiting for the word, and then they would be coming in and where would that leave us? By the look of these guys in the yard it would be "up dung river without a paddle". The 'Strikers', well they weren't even standing up. They were just all sitting around there in the yard as if it was Christmas or some blasted thing, and I start to say to myself, "Well Gees, if the bastards do come in, there is no organisation here whatsoever". So with no further ado I take the initiative, and I start to walk up and down and am talking to these guys like this – "Hey you guys, liven up! If these pissant bs get the word to come in here off the Governor to bash us, well don't just sit there like a lot of dumb arseholes and cop it sweet. No sir! Get on your frigging feet and get ready. We fight! OK? You get the idea! No fear! We don't just defend ourselves against these turds with their frigging little nightsticks! No sir-ee Bob! We do better than that, a whole bloody lot better! We get the bastards around the frigging legs and when they go down, we jump on their frigging skulls, we punch the bastards in the head and we kick their frigging teeth right down their f-all stupid screw bloody throats; you dig me guys? You get my drift here?"

And straight away they clamber to their feet and start to prick up their ears, because they like what they hear and I can tell that I have whetted their thirst for blood real good and they say, "Yeah! Bob! Like keep talking man! Clue us in, kid!" So I do, and I start to tell them, "Look, if they start to come in, we'll stand and pair off about four or five in a bunch and if a screw bastard comes at you well, lay him low".

There are a lot more of us than there are of them. And by this time the whole yard is standing around and are listening to what I am saying. So there I am, standing there just as if I am that master sergeant I spoke about before, or even Knute Rockne coaching Notre Dame Football squad.

So then I can see at a glance that my words have made a real healthy impression on these guys and they have their fists clenched and murder in their eyes, and I am thinking all of a sudden, *"Well, if they do come in – well f them! There will be a nice few widows at home, grieving for their screw bastard husbands tomorrow"* and I tell the other guys this, and I get replies like "My frigging oath!" and "You bloody well bet!" and the whites of their knuckles are standing out through their clenched fists and inwardly I am singing praises to God (O God, have mercy on me for my delusions!), like King David for having furnished me with the ability to turn this bunch of docile patsies into a first rate murder squad, just waiting for the kill.

Well, for some dumb reason or other, I don't know why (it sure as heck would have been a glorious confrontation), it never eventuated. I suppose after all that tension and mental priming, preparing ourselves for the fray, I must have been a bit disappointed, but then again, maybe not, it could have been a bloody and disastrous ordeal for everyone concerned, including me. The Governor must have told them to hang off and wait.

The time kept on ticking past, as time does have a habit of doing – and after a while it was dark. We weren't quitters and I myself was all for carrying on with a worthwhile endeavour. Some guys said, "We'll stay here till we get certain promises from the Governor", so we kept waiting – I think most guys could see and agreed by this time that if this was the case we might have a long wait on our hands and already most (or all) of us were getting tired and quite cold and shivering and wishing that we were in bed or listening to the radio or something of this kind.

So after a while there was some amount of discussion with Max and Doc and the rest, and Max said to me, "What do you say, Hughie?" So I said.

"Well I figure if we go in now it might be better for us all. In any case we have got our point across to the bastards". So Max said, "OK, then it's unanimous, that we go in now. Is everyone agreed?" and everyone said.

"Yeah!" So we went in to our cells.

I thought that they had promised us no reprisals. "Well so much for the word of a screw or the Governor". They let us sleep until daybreak and then in they came and it was "action at the station". We were all hauled out and told to get ready, which we hastily did. Then they had us paired off and handcuffed, we were being shanghaied (sent on a special escort to some unknown destination without being given any notice or reason why). Of course we all knew why. Somebody had told me that Max and Doc had got sent off already, to either Bathurst or Grafton. They had myself and about five others singled out for being leaders in the plot and soon we were heading back to Long Bay, but at this time we didn't know the destination.

Well, anyhow, when we got back there, to the "Bay" they shoved us all in Yard 13 of the MRP "Front Yards". They had these yards in all the maximum security sections of all prisons, and were there for the housing of any prisoners who were segregated from the others for punishment reasons.

Well, then they would be put in some special wing, and through the day they would be placed in the "Front Yards".

So we were shoved into Yard 13 to cool our heels until the authorities decided what they were going to do with us but it was no big deal. We all had a fair idea of that or so we hoped anyway. These "front yards" were kind of like big lion cages that you might find in any zoo. I was a bit surprised that we had not been given a heavy serve for our participation in the Goulburn Riot, particularly since they had us singled out as "main instigators". Maybe Turnbull might have been a man of his word, after all and this might have been the extent of his "no reprisals" promise. But still he hadn't been one hundred percent faithful to his promise – because we had been "shanghaied" after all.

They kept us all in 13 Yard for about a fortnight, pacing about like some kind of wild animals (that's what we were, in their estimation I suppose). There were myself, Johnny Parker, "the Yank" and about three or four others whose names I have forgotten after all this time.

Well like I was saying, there we were pacing backwards and forwards, but we managed to keep each other laughing and in good spirits by reminding each other of the "underfed dogs" looks that these Goulburn screws had had and how disappointed we all were when the "*ding dong* go" and "Donnybrook" at· the finish had not eventuated. We also made each other feel hardy and strong by saying to each other how we wouldn't worry about what they were going to do with us, but how we would "cop it on the chin" whatever happened, and so forth and so on. However, we were pretty sure that something would have to "break" pretty soon. We didn't have very long to wait for the "break" and I soon found out that I had been reclassified, this time for the "Parra".

Parramatta Gaol

No I didn't really know what to expect from being sent to Parramatta, but I was glad that it wasn't Bathurst or Grafton (the fear, for I suppose that is what it was, though I tried to convince myself differently) had gone through my mind, more than once. So now that I had been told it was "Parra", well, I felt a whole lot more "at ease" to say the least. It was as though someone had lifted the weight of three or four elephants and half a dozen semi-trailers off my mind.

Of course I had heard about the Parramatta Circle and other things connected with the "good old days" of convict correction that made me glad that it was 1970 and not 1935.

The Parramatta "Circle" for intractables still did exist, but basically "Parra" had the reputation of being a "pretty good" gaol where a long time crim like myself could settle down and get along with doing his time in peace that is all I really wanted.

They put us in two wagons, which did not have any windows. I couldn't see out. Gees! That did "shit" me. I was trying to keep my bearings in relationship to the "compass" (the lay of the land) and I could feel the wretched wagon turning this way and that, and going around this corner and that, and so on till I started to feel like some vegetable that had just been torn out by the roots. You see, I must explain here, that from the time the cops had taken me away from home, I had always been able to keep my bearings in regard to the lay of the land.

This was to me and would be to most people, I imagine, important, to know just where you are facing, but when you are behind four walls, it is not so easy, of course, when they were shipping me north and south from Goulburn, well that helped a lot, and I knew where I was then – but now I was leaving the "Bay" and they had me in this wretched "Bun Wagon" where I couldn't see out. Well I felt like a one legged man in a backside kicking contest, completely blooming helpless.

But at last we reached Parramatta and they let us out. I managed to tell myself, "Don't worry about your bearings for now, forget about which way is which and after you have settled in here and get the feel of the joint, well, your natural instincts will tell where is where". And it must have been good advice I gave myself there, because after a while my spirit did seem to feel the area out and everything was OK. I must explain to people reading here also that crims never get to see the stars unless it is through their cell window, because mostly they are always locked up about four to five pm daily, but to a crim doing a long time, well the stars that are visible would probably be the best way of keeping "tabs" on your direction.

Well Long Bay had size and Goulburn had height, but this Parramatta seemed to have the lot, and a certain amount of historical quality thrown in for good measure. I can understand how people who have had great cultural experience and travelled the world and seen marvellous things may scoff at me, but I am telling it to you straight, you square heads from outside who don't know what a crims life is like.

I tell you straight, this Parramatta Gaol had a lot of godforsaken history of its own to boast about, and I reckon a lot of human spirit and anguish and whatever else must have been poured out behind these sandstone slab walls over the years since it was built. And exactly how much, not you nor I, but only God himself will ever really know, that is for sure, and I think that when I had looked through this place, something inside me must have said, "Well, Bob, you may not have seen everything, but maybe you have seen enough and a darn lot more than you realise".

I wasn't alone at "Parra". I met a lot of guys that I had known over the years, mostly from Goulburn and they seemed pleased to see me again as well.

I was housed up in 5 wing. I forget who was the wing screw there at 5 wing at the time. I didn't take too much notice, these Parramatta screws were all foreign to me. Now and again I'd see a screw who I had known from Goulburn and he would greet me with a friendly, "Hello Hughie, when did you get here?" or something like this. I would make a friendly reply. Lots of these screws weren't bad people. I didn't bother to explain about the Goulburn ordeal. I figured that they would probably find out of their own accord anyway.

They (the authorities) had given permission to paint the whole gaol, right throughout. So the crims, who were not working on other jobs, set to with tooth and nail, to paint the whole place – the insides of all the wings and all the cells, right throughout the whole prison, with beautiful exterior enamel ultra-gloss wall paint. It really transformed the whole place and gave it a kind of "Walt Disney fairyland" look. Anyway everything certainly looked a lot cleaner and brighter.

They even let the crims (a lot of them possessed very admirable artistic talent) paint landscapes and murals of wild geese and grazing cattle and ships at sea and even religious scenes of the crucifixion, and the nativity and the annunciation all over the inside walls of various Wings, and in their own cells if they so desired. The whole darn prison there became one huge gigantic work of art. You would have to see it all to believe it. I even got the feeling that some of these guys may have been making some kind of dedication to Jesus by putting all this most remarkable effort into these "expressions of spiritualism" as an atonement for things that they had done wrong in the past and felt sorry for.

I was put to work in the laundry with Slim and Shorty and Vince. This Vince had red hair. Is Vince a special name given to guys with red hair? I don't know, I had known a couple who did have. So anyway, my job was to deliver the clean laundry in trollies (big white laundry bags full) and to pick up the dirty laundry and to bring it back to the laundry for washing. It was not a bad job either, and I got to go everywhere, right throughout the whole prison. All the different wings and all the workshops.

I met Paddy O'Niel, one day and he said, "Here Bob" and he pushed a small package into my hand wrapped up in grease-proof paper. I opened it and there were three hardboiled eggs. I started to thank him, and he just said "Don't worry about it, Hughie, that's what friends are for", and, "If you want any more just come and tell me". I liked Paddy, he reminded me a lot of my cousin Stephen, but I didn't want to impose too much on him about the eggs. I knew he was "working hot" somewhere in order to get them, but I certainly enjoyed the three that he gave me.

They got permission after a while to build a boxing ring. A lot of the lads were keen on the sport, so the authorities agreed it would be a good way in allowing the lads to "let off a bit of steam" and who knows maybe they could build some budding "pros" as well; anyway the crims all loved it. It was all in fun and some good bouts were staged by some of the more "willing" types (the aboriginal lads were greatly interested and when they agreed to get the ring put up well lots of the "abbo" boys said that "things are so good here now I don't want to get out, my missus will only nag me to death anyway".

Old Lucky – Lucky Starr, the singer from the fifties came in and would tutor the crims who were interested in learning different things and playing techniques, on their guitars. I say "old", because at this time he looked a fair bit more mature for his years, than the smooth faced young boy that used to strum out Rock n Roll songs on "*Bandstand*" and "*Six o'clock Rock*".

BIBLE?

I met up with Col Anderson again at Parra. Col was a Lifer and a damned good guitar player. I had known him from Goulburn. A tall, good looking guy with a fair Aryan complexion and blue eyes. He was also a real sober and sensible guy to talk to; there was no "mug lair" in Col. Whenever he spoke, he spoke very soberly. Col was also a Bible reader at the time. I didn't know this at first but not till later. So, as it was then that I started reading the Bible, and I knew without too much working out that this was my

Book. There were plenty of Bibles placed by the Gideons so that there would be enough in the Gaol, so that every crim could have one in his cell if he wanted it, but hardly anyone used to bother to read them, indeed, there was myself and Col and a friend of his whose name I have forgotten and we were the only ones who were really devoted to reading it. So I started reading it closely, hanging on every written word as it were, and absorbing as much of it as I could as I went.

I started reading it from the first word of the Genesis and I was determined not to stop till I had reached the finish. I would carry my Bible everywhere at the weekend – as would Col, and we'd find a nice quiet place somewhere in one of the yards (the whole of Parramatta Gaol was "open" at the weekends and inmates were allowed to wander wherever they wanted to) and sit down to do a bit of deep reading.

I remember I used to hold my Bible up sometimes on the evening muster and sing out to Col and say, "Hey Col, look brother, God's Holy word, the greatest treasure in the world, and only you and me to appreciate it", and Col would make a reply like "That's it Hughie, well you know what they say about there being none so blind as those who refuse to see!" and so we'd talk like this to each other. The other guys would all "pay out" on us and snort and we'd get remarks like "frigging Bible Bashers" and "Bloody Ratbags" and so on. They couldn't understand it at all, the 'poor dumb bastards'.

So, after that, like I have said, I used to read my Bible, just about all the time, whenever I had a spare moment, and still do! Once a Bible reader always a Bible reader. I could never explain it exactly, but once you find the treasure there in the

"Good Book", well, you get a whole new lease on life. It's food for the hungry and a well of life for the thirsty, and I knew as long as I had this book, "the word of God", well, they could build all the stone walls around me they wanted to, I couldn't care less. It used to amuse me to see how much amusement all these other guys were getting from seeing me always with my head stuck in the "Good Book". Lots of these guys, even guys I had known for years, used to have "shots" at me, and poke fun at me for this. I didn't care.

I tried to explain to them just how good it was, but for the most part, my efforts fell on deaf ears, so after a while, I decided to give up trying. I could see it was just a case of those who are given the grace of seeing the treasure, or those who just refuse it when it's right there in front of them.

I would have been very content to stay there at Parra, and sit around and read my Bible, but after I had spent a couple of years working in the laundry, I got wind that they were fixing to send me back to the "Bay", the reason being as I understood it, was to give me a series of psychological assessment tests from time to time. I was pleased to hear that something was "In the wind" and Col said to me "Hughie, you're fixed mate! This is the best news you could ever hope to get. It means that they are summing you up for consideration pending your release, Pal, so try to look a little enthusiastic". Then he said, "Look! Make sure that when this 'Psycho' guy sees you and asks you questions that you tell him exactly what you think he wants to hear, do this all the time, and you'll be sitting pretty, do you get my drift, Pal?"

That Col, he was nobody's fool that's for sure.

One smart cookie, that's what he was. He wasn't about to give this advice to anyone, just to me on account of how we were 'Buddies'. He told me this personally.

I said, "Yeah. Thanks Col", and I could see straight away that this was real good advice to keep in the back of my brain, as I prepared myself for these interviews, that lay ahead.

So they sent me back to the "Bay" and when I got there at the MRP they housed me up in 10 Wing for remands. I was to work there as a "sweeper". Kevin Hoppins was "Head Sweeper" at the time, then Chappo, Nev, Jackson, Geoff, myself, Barry, Gold Thorpe, Alan Regan and "Ross" – who didn't stay long. We worked under "Mr Usher". Brian Usher was the wing officer and one spot on, decent bloke for a Pommie, a fair man with a dry sense of humour, a family man. He showed us photos of his wife and sons, and himself when he had been in the New Zealand army in his younger days and of an evening when the others were having their tea, we would gather around and swap a few laughs and Brian would tell us about some of his "more hectic" moments at home.

But for the most part we were kept pretty busy, and we kept 10 Wing really clean and shining, with the floor all stained and polished with black marking ink and wax, polished with the electric polisher, till it shone like glass. Brian would say to the regulars when they would come in the wing. "See that floor my sweepers have done. If any one of you bludgers so much as puts a mark on it, well I'll give you a week in solitary on nought but bread and water" and he wasn't smiling when he said it either!!

Our duties were to do that: to keep the wing shiny, polished and clean, the brass fittings, the padlocks, and the door bolts all were sandpapered, oiled and so on. We issued the sugar and milk ration, poured the boiling hot tea out of the big copper tea urns in every doorway before meals and dished the meals out to the inmates as they came in. Then we'd have to collect the used dixies and cutlery from door to door afterward, accompanied by a screw.

It was also the duty of a sweeper to assist by cleaning up after the screws, whenever there was a "ramp" on.

There were two kinds of "Ramps" (cell searches). The first was the usual routine search that was always on once or twice a week no matter what. The second was the special "surprise" or "heavy" Ramp that was supposed to come as a big surprise to everybody.

It never was (a surprise I mean). The word from the prison grapevine just couldn't be competed with. Some guy in the office would be pussy-footing around, and hear the screws talking and "bingo" before you could say "Darcy Dugan now an altar boy", well, we'd all know what was going to happen, long before it did. But they never knew that we knew, that was always the way it was. It must have saved the backsides of a lot of guys. We (the sweepers) would get the word, that there was going to be a surprise "ramp" on somebody and straight away one of us would toe it up the stairs and tip the guy off, so that when they came in, well, he would be prepared for the worst. It used to amuse the heck out of me to see how these 'dumb screws' would come in the wing so serious and still thinking that their secret Ramp was still a secret.

They would get their hammers out, and bang all the bars and tear everything to pieces real good, usually looking for a "shiv", a homemade knife, or some homemade weapon or tool, probably in connection with a tip off that some crim, or inmate, was intending to perpetrate an escape bid, or something of this nature. Or sometimes it might be that they got tipped off that some guy would have a "shiv" and planning on using it on somebody the next day. These kinds of things did happen from time to time, usually when two guys, "toughs" or "heavies", would get jealous of each other's reputation, or when some guy would try to "bump off" some child molester or child killer or something of this nature, and set himself up as an "avenging angel of death". But the most popular motive in prison would be the "reputation" or "jealousy" theme. I had a pal once whom I hid a "shiv" for, I will just call him Russel. I hid this "shiv" in a special hiding place. They came in and turned the whole place upside down, looking for it, searching high and low. Little did they know that I had hid it for my buddy Russ, and knew exactly where it was. I didn't know what he wanted it for and I didn't care. He was my pal, and that was all the reason I needed. Would he have done the same for me? I think so.

Us sweepers, we didn't have any boxing gloves and we wanted to spar – boxing facilities had not been agreed to yet, not at Long Bay anyway. So we got this Drag Queen, who used to work on a sewing machine in 5 Shop to run us up a pair of boxing gloves. All the drags and queens and transvestites and "poofs" and you name it were housed in 9 Wing and went to work in 5 Shop. Also, it housed the ones marked "On Protection" and those whose cards were marked NA (non-associate). They all went to work in 5 shop, sorting out spare prison clothing and repairing it. Some of the "spunkier" looking pieces used to take female hormones and I have seen some of these come and go with makeup on that would make Farrah Fawcett and Raquel Welch eat their heart out. You may laugh at this but let me say here and now that you would have to see it to really believe it. They would bask in all the attention that they would get from the ordinary crims, who hadn't seen real females for a long spell and who would whistle at them and, make "catcalls" etc.

These queens would smile in a movie magazine kind of way and wiggle their behinds and blow kisses and wave (while going to and from work) and when they were on their way to the shower block, they would nearly provoke a bloody riot, with their long hair, painted finger and toenails and mascaraed eyelashes. It was a real circus that was for sure.

Lots of guys there would just about break their necks for an opportunity to go a message or something to 5 Shop.

The Slot Thief

Now in 10 wing where I was, we had taken some serious notice that somebody was thieving stuff out of the cells (our "slots"), at times when crims would be allowed in the wing for various reasons such as to clean up your cell or to take a shower or things like this. Well for some time different inmates had been coming and complaining to us sweepers that stuff in their cells had been "going off", but up till now, we had been unable to solve the mystery.

So we were getting quite agitated to say the least, but we kept our eyes and ears open and watched everyone intently – no matter who they were or for what reason they came in. A "slot thief" in an environment like prison is a guy who should realise better that if he does not stop doing what he is doing, well then when he gets caught it will be the worse for him. In jail, the 'Honour among thieves' Law still holds to a large extent and the unwritten rule is: 'No crim thieves off another crim'. The repercussion, if not observed, can be violent, and not very pretty sometimes. Also the culprits can expect no mercy from screws in these kind of incidents. They will turn their backs and let the crims themselves carry out their own vigilante type justice.

So we kept expressively vigilant in our efforts to find this guy, whoever he was, because we could see, by the constant array of missing and stolen stuff that this guy was becoming more and more confident, as he went along, that he was in the clear and wouldn't t be found out – that's what he thought.

So we had narrowed our list of suspects down to this one particular guy and we knew now that we wouldn't have long to wait, so we concentrated all our attentions on him. He was a 'wog', a 'chocco' (chocolate frog), a German or a Czech or something, but he wasn't a Yugoslav, I was pretty sure of that. I had known several Yugoslavs since I had been in gaol and all of the ones I had known would have been too morally scrupulous to slot thieve. I think he may have been a Czech. Anyway, this Milos (that was his name) had come into the wing, to fix his cell up or some such an excuse or so he told us, and as he often did do, prior to the event of something mysteriously "going off" from somebody's cell, so we knew now, with very little doubt, that this was our guy. All we had to do was to keep vigilant and catch the "son of a bitch" in the act.

So this time, after giving him a bit of a head start we followed him up onto the landing and (no worries) there the 'son of a bitch' was creeping along the landing and looking into this cell and that, to see if he could find a "fair cop". All of a sudden, our long spent time was answered. He went into this other guy's cell to help himself. We sprung like blood-hounds to the kill, all of us and filed into the cell after him, one behind the other and I think it was "Chappo" who said, "Doing a little bit of thieving, eh mate?"

Well you should have seen the expression on this guy's face as he turned around, I think it must have been panic mixed with fear and guilt and frustration thrown in for good measure. He knew he was in for something but as yet he didn't know exactly what! But he whined like a wounded dog as we dragged or shoved him down to see the screw. The screw in charge was some tall lanky guy who was filling in for Brian, as it was his day off.

He was whining like a stuck pig and we hadn't even touched the "son of a gun" yet. "Milos no do nothing. Milos no take anything", and all this darn nonsense. It just added to our anger. Gees! After thieving off these guys for all of this time and then getting caught, well you would think that this noble, European unmentionable would have displayed a bit of backbone, and take it like a man. So anyway, we showed him to the screw, who sat there in his chair and scrutinised this character very carefully from top to bottom and from bottom to top. Then he gets up and closing the wing doors and padlocking them, he says to us "OK, well it's up to you sweepers. You can do what you like, but don't mess the wing up too much, will you?"

Milos whined again and looked none too happy to say the least, so we decided we would try and get him at ease, so as we are dragging him down to the far end cell we are buttering him up and saying, "Look Milos, we are all your friends here", and, "We just want to talk to you pal", and all stuff like this. Well after a while this look of relief starts to creep over his face and that's when the action starts. Somebody bounces a right hook right across his teeth and a left to follow. Well, two or three of us all moved in and followed in a likewise manner, and by now Milos has a bleeding nose and a black eye. But our thirst for the distribution of justice has not been quenched yet, so as he goes down on the ground, screaming "blue murder" we started to kick the heck out of him. So we carry on kicking the nonsense out of him for a minute or two. He was lucky! Lucky that us sweepers all wore thongs, so the kicking he got was hardly enough to give him a decent bruising.

But it was enough to hurt the so-and-so's dignity to the point of teaching him a lesson.

So most of us were surprised when he had enough "go" left in him to struggle to his feet then and after lunging through the cell doorway to run all the way up the wing where he proceeded to rattle the doors, which the screw had locked. The screw grabbed this guy by the collar and said "Look you bastard; these sweepers here have let you off, lightly. If it was me I would break your bloody neck. This is Australia. Understand? We are men here, not flipping arseholes, and we don't steal from each other under these kinds of conditions. Now do you understand that you bloody wog bastard?" The fellow nodded, he was still too afraid to speak. Ha! He understood all right. The wing screw undid the locks and let him out into the yard.

There was a fair amount of indecision among the sweepers as to whether a bleeding nose, a blackened eye, a cut lip and a set of well bruised ribs was good enough, and most of us, myself included, were all for taking him back down the wing and giving the so-and-so a second helping, but it was getting near to evening muster time so this wing screw said to us, "It will have to do for now. I think he's learnt his lesson!" So, as it turned out there was no more thieving and all the crims in the wing that learned about what had happened agreed that the situation had been admirably dealt with.

New Guys

One day, not so long after the slot thieving episode there came a new bunch of guys, all new, and on remand, to be housed in W Wing. Among them there was this little Asiatic guy, quite frail in statute, and he looked as though he had all the cares of existence burdened upon his shoulders – in fact he was really doing it as hard as anyone I ever have seen. But there was nothing I could do for him. In fact, he hardly spoke any English at all. So a week or thereabouts went past, and I could see, day by day, that he was living in sheer hell (I don't know why, if he had only told himself to toughen up and endure the situation. Usually these Chinese types, like to revel in their reputation as being tough enduring types able to cope with anything). Anyway to get on with the story: – One evening, as the fellows were piling into the wing as usual and picking their dixies of tucker up and making their way up to the landing to their slots, this little Asiatic guy takes it upon himself to dive over the handrail down between the space between the handrail and the net (they had hung, as they always did, this net along in the centre of the wing in between both sides of the landing and it was supposed to stop guys from falling over). But in this case, as I have said, the guy was small and frail, and he dove down through the gap which was about 9–12 inches. Some other fellow grabbed him by his trousers but they came off and he fell out of them and crashed down onto his skull, and his skull can't have been too hard, because by all accounts, it cracked like an eggshell and he bled to death there all over Brian's lovely black marking ink and wax floor. I have heard of people diving or falling from much greater heights than this but apparently this guy wanted to end it all so that may (or may not) have made all the difference.

Well, poor guy, but at least he was successful in his attempt and went quickly. He was Chinese, I think, not a Jap but we all decided to give him the honourable title of the "Kamikaze diver", anyway and then set about cleaning up his blood with dustpans and brushes.

Soon after this episode, they told me to pack what gear I had and to get ready to go down to the CIP for a spell.

There was no explanation of why, but after having already done so long in gaol, I couldn't be bothered asking them "why?" I just did it. It was all the same to me; let the so-and-sos send me where they wanted to, I couldn't care less. Blast them anyway!

So I went down to the CIP and they told me I was to be housed up in 4 Wing, where Cummo was the wing officer. "Cummo", Mr Cummings, was a ruddy round faced man with a beer gut, which told that he was in his 40s or thereabouts. But from what I had been told he had been a pretty fair sort of amateur boxer in his younger days probably before he became a screw.

Most of the crims in the CIP liked Cummo and he had the good reputation as being the kind of screw that you could confide in or talk to with a fair amount of confidence if you had a problem. He was all for helping a crim out if he possibly could.

The old gallows was there down at the end of 4 Wing.

The trap door and apparatus were clearly visible from the floor.

It used to be operated by a steel lever that was inserted down through a slot in the steel landing adjacent to the trap door, and in between the condemned cells, one on the right side of the landing and one on the left. Cummo still had the lever in his office, and I had been told by some of the older guys that had been in the wing for a fair while, that the screws used to give it an oil and a run through every so often, just to keep it operational.

But now, or recently, they must have been told not to bother, because the thing was never used.

Cummo told me that now it was just a relic of the hard old days of the "Bay" and best forgotten. I believed him, just to look at the damned thing made a person want to loosen your collar.

On each side of the gallows trap were the two condemned cells (you could still use these cells to sleep in if you wanted to). Some crims did, but for my part the atmosphere of death and execution was still all too clearly present around these formidable relics of the past. The condemned cells, one on the right and one on the left looked the same as any of the other cells from the outside, the difference was: as you went in through the main cell door to the condemned cells, about two feet inside the door were a row of steel bars with another barred door right across the full width of the cell, and across the space in between the wall and the bars was a seat, where the prison officer would have to sit all night and keep a vigilant watch on the condemned man, till they came along to read him the Last Rites and carry out the sentence. Usually about 6 am in the morning.

I was assisting around in the "Boys' Shop" at the time (working that is) together with my friend Ziggy (a Pole who I had known from Goulburn). I am pretty sure Zig was also a GP (General Practice) doctor. These younger guys, most of whom were still in their teens, looked up to Zig and myself because we were old lags who had been through the mill (so to speak) and as for myself, I didn't mind working with these nice young kids either and offering some advice and help to them wherever I could. I stayed on working in the Boys Shop for a spell, and on Sunday I didn't have anything much to do so I started to attend the Catholic Mass, mostly out of curiosity, but also because I used to like this pretty young Nun, Sister Carmel who used to come into the Gaol and walk around talking to the various crims who would be locked up in the yards. Sister Germanus, the little silver haired doll of a nun, would go with her. Lots of the guys who probably didn't know Germanus' name would call her "Tiny".

Germanus died sometime later. She would have been well on in years. She must have been missed greatly by anyone who had known her. Well, I started to learn all about the Catholic Faith, and I learned where the Roman Catholic Church was the one and only true Christian Church, and its history went all the way back to St Peter the Apostle of Jesus Christ, and even to Christ himself. I never knew this, and I was pretty sure that my mum and dad never knew it either. Any institution that goes all the way back to Christ our Lord and God, can't be argued with. So, after Ziggy had said to me to go and see the Catholic Chaplain in Prison about becoming baptised, I thought to myself "*Yes*" to become a part of the true Church, is a step, that I can only be glad about forever. So I did it.

The Teacup

The Catholic Chaplain at the time was Father William Meacham. He had been the chaplain there at the "Bay" for a long time, about 30 years I think, and had seen them all come and go with the exception of Ned Kelly maybe. I told him I wanted to become a Catholic and after a bit of speculation, interrogation and instruction, he had to agree. So he said "Yeah! OK, Hughie, come and see me over in my office this arvo about 3 pm". So, I did and after sitting me down in a chair and going through the ceremony briefly (the Creed) and asking me whether I believed in all those things, he took a teacup full of water and blessed it, made the sign of the cross with the water three times on my forehead. "I baptise you, in the Name of the Father and of the Son and of the Holy Spirit!" And that was it! I was declared one of the flock. I can't tell anyone how good and blessed and sanctified and everything I felt about it. So, that is how I came to be a Roman Catholic, and if I do say so myself, up to this present day, a pretty conscientious one at that. In a place like Prison, you just can't imagine how tranquil a feeling one gets, when one is able to attend the Holy Eucharist and Communion and go to Confession.

Sister Carmel and my friend Zig congratulated me and told me how pleased they were for me.

Well, after some period of time thereafter, I was told, that they were sending me out to the Management and Training Corporation (MTC) Prison so that I could have a spell in a minimum security environment. Things were supposed to be much more "at home" out there or so they reckoned, but I had heard the "screws" refer to it as Disneyland. So whatever they meant by that, I didn't know, but it made me a bit sceptical, but "theirs not to reason why" as Lord Tennyson once wrote, so with no more ado, I packed up my gear and prepared for the worst.

Well as it so happened the "worst" wasn't too bad at all and I was surprised, to be honest. It was the newest section of Long Bay yet to be completed, and was made with all the special attention and improvement that was supposed to transform a maximum security prison to a home away from home. But for a little while I was doubtful, I thought that I would feel like a fish out of water.

But like I said it turned out pretty good this MTC section, and I started to like the feel of the joint, and to get into the groove if you know what I mean. It certainly had most of the comforts of home with cobblestoned paths, gardens, walkways, football and cricket playing fields, a basket-ball court and dining rooms in each of the wings where you could sit down and eat your meals and even watch TV while you ate.

They also had nice little bedrooms instead of the old stone cells of the CIP. You could make your own request for any job that you felt you could do at and if there were any vacancies in that section well you would probably get the job, if you were an inmate of normal intelligence.

I had heard that they needed cooks in the MTC kitchens, so I applied for a cook's job and I was told "Yeah! OK, but you have got to start from the bottom of the ladder".

It's the normal routine that they all have to follow. You have got to get to "know the ropes". So I said "Yeah! OK, Pal, Shoot me the white threads man! I'm here to make a big impression". The clerk gave me a funny look, but he wrote down 'kitchen hand', in his book and went away to get me my white "clobber" and heavy rubberised kitchen boots. Then I was shown the special wing where us cooks were housed. All the kitchen and cookhouse staff was housed in the one special wing. So I was shown to my cell or "room" and started in there along with a couple of new "dudes" who were just starting as well.

So as the clerk guy had said, we had to start right from rock bottom as everybody did, and that meant as a "slushie" washing up the dishes and whatever. Also us cooks, all of us, we all had to get up real early, about 5 am and start the early jobs that had to be done. There was milk to be measured out, and porridge to be cooked and distributed into dixies, tea to be made, other jobs to be prepared "early". Sometimes I would have to sit down and peel two or more whole bags of onions. It was a job most guys would try and palm off onto somebody if they possibly could.

They had this huge cauldron there that they would use at clean-up time. It was hinged, so it could be tipped up and the contents would pour out everywhere, all over the kitchen floor and all of us would set to with squeegees and scrubbers along with heaps of grease cutting carbolic soap powder to make the place clean once more. Like I said, the big cauldron had a tip up base with swivel wheels with rubber tyres underneath, and when it was filled to the brim with boiling hot carbolic soapy water, we'd sing out, "Look out!" Two or three of us (all in our bare feet) would jump on the side of the "trolley" the rest would push, then we'd send the big cauldron (with the guys standing and hanging onto the side like "grim death") careering down the kitchen floor and when we reached about halfway or a bit more down the floor, we'd jump off and tip it up, and boiling hot soapy water would go everywhere all over the floor. It really used to cut into the grease and fat, which at times was quite thick along with other rubbish across the floor, but there were also big spill-ways and drain-ways right across the floor so it wasn't long before we had everything as clean as a whistle once more.

The kitchen floor was all of red tiles and had to be kept hygienically clean. The inspections would come every so often to make sure everything was up to scratch.

The fringe benefits for anyone working as a staff member in the kitchen were unreal. You could help yourself to whatever you wanted and I could hear myself saying to myself, "Gees! Bob! How come it took you all of these years until you finally put in for a kitchen job? I could've been living in the laps of luxury". As well as being able to get all the fresh fruit we wanted, there was also steak, kidneys, mushrooms, eggs, and even specially baked custard tarts and chocolate eclairs and French pastries and turnovers that were cooked especially for the screws by the pastry cooks. There was always heaps of these left over, so we could take whatever we wanted.

The regular meals improved over the years for the regular guys as well, I am happy to be able to report, and in the latter years, crims were eating as well as most people outside – better in lots of cases – with baked lamb dinner, crumbed cutlets, corned beef, fish fillets, all done with vegetables and or white sauce or gravy – and desserts – like wine trifle or fruit salad and ice cream, two or three times a week. Also the breakfast menu was updated and the inmates would get minced kidney on toast or spaghetti and meat balls, or bacon and eggs as well as the normal selection of Corn Flakes, Rice Bubbles or Weet-Bix, replacing the old corn mush or oatmeal porridge. For my money, the old oatmeal porridge (though they did away with it) was, and always will be, the most sustaining tucker ever served in a NSW Prison. But despite this vast improvement in food, very few crims sounded happily satisfied.

Of course lots of guys wanted us to traffic stuff for them and they would offer us all sorts of things like "grouse tobacco" and such like. We really wanted to help them out too and would have willingly done so, but of course if you were caught trafficking (a kitchen staff member that is), well, of course, you would lose your job for sure.

I got to the second kitchen stage before I left, and that was trolley man looking after these electric trollies, or "Hot Boxes" as they were called. They were all made entirely of stainless steel and had racks and steel dish compartments in them, where all the different kinds of food would be put separately and then the Hot Boxes would be wheeled to all the various sections of the prison, to all the various wings to be distributed to the prison inmates.

My job then as a trolley man was to clean, look after at least one trolley and clean it right out thoroughly at morning, at noon, and at evening.

So I stayed there working in the MTC Kitchen for some time, till I was transferred to work in the bookbinders, and then one day not too long after, I was told I was going back to the main section again, so the old moving trick was on again.

Changes

I went back to A Wing and Cummo told me I was going up the MRP the following day, and he said to me, "Good news, Hughie They want you up at the MRP. It's to front the Parole Board, from what I hear, so make sure you put on some nice clean clobber, mate! Shave and try and make a good impression". Then he added, "This could be it, Bob. You've done a long time and now it looks like you could be on your way out, so good luck", I said. "Thanks, Cummo", and shook his hand which he offered to me. Then I hurried up to my cell to get my stuff together ready to go the following morning.

So I didn't get all that much sleep that night and I kept thinking, "At last, after all this time!" But then I started thinking, "Blast it! That outside world! What is it going to be like after all this time?" And the 'wonderful Dream' seemed somewhat less agreeable.

Anyway the next day came, and I thanked Cummo once again and a couple of other guys including Ziggy and Darcy Dugan. He was there at the time and I used to spend a lot of time walking in the yard and talking to Darcy about the old days, the hard years at Grafton when they had done everything they could to break his spirit and failed. He was a very likeable little guy was Darcy. Smart, but in a sensible way, not a skite or a braggart. He seemed pretty fit for his age, but grey haired and starting to feel his years, I dare say.

So I said "Auf Wiedersehen" to these people and departed for the MRP. – I didn't have very long to wait, because the Parole Board wanted to see me, the very next day and when it came around, there was good old Bob (me) looking very bright eyed and bushy tailed. So they called me in to front before the Board which consisted of a couple of Senior Prison Officers, whom I had known pretty well over the years. A nice looking mature and very sexy looking lady therapist, a Chinese Social Worker, Richard Zee, who I had known for a long time and some other guy from the Parole Board.

These people "stood" as the Parole Council and told me that they were here to question me in regard to my being released on "license" (a five year one). The sexy looking dame was doing all the talking and she said to me, "How does this idea seem to you, Mr Cox?" I must have been a million miles away, but actually it was this parole dame that had me going, she was so gorgeous. She was seated behind the desk, so I couldn't see her legs, worse luck, but if they were anything like the rest of her – well they must have been close to perfect. She had blonde hair done up high and blue-green eyes and spoke with a definite air of authority. I had brief visions of her in black leather and standing over me with stilt heeled shoes and a whip. I must have had a faraway look on my face, as I gazed into those beautiful aquamarine eyes. She spoke again, "Mr Cox?"

"Eh? Yeah. Eh? I beg your pardon?"

I was trying to gather my senses. She sat forward with a smile and an amused look on her face. I felt like a drongo. She spoke once more. "Now how does that sound, Robert?" she said. "A five-year license would be the conditions, You would have to see the parole officer from time to time".

I felt like saying, "Yeah! Sweetheart, that's just Jake! So long as I can spent the first 100 or so nights on a couch cuddling you". But I didn't.

So I just said, "Yes, Ma'am that would be real fine, thank you".

She said, "Well, Mr Zee will give you all the details".
Richard Zee was a friend of mine, after when he was talking to me alone, he said to me, "For a moment there I thought you were going to jump over the table and rape her", I said. "Yeah, well, don't think that the thought was absent. She certainly was a good-looker!" He laughed at that.

They released me soon after and everyone wanted to shake my hand and tell me "Good luck". The conditions, besides, were that I should stay as an "outpatient" at Callan Park Mental Hospital. The reports I had heard about Callan Park Hospital from the "good old days" of years gone by were pretty grim, though things were supposed to be a lot different and better now. So I started thinking well, maybe this Callan Park joint will make an ex-crim like myself feel real "at home".

So they housed me up in ward 4–5 there and it wasn't too bad. I even had a girlfriend, Jenny, Jenny D. She knew that I'd been in gaol for a long time and she was nice and friendly to me. We'd hold hands sometimes, or maybe sometimes I'd cuddle her a bit, she didn't mind. She told me that she wasn't trying to lead me on, but, apart from that, it wasn't a sexual relationship. I knew that Jenny had had a hard life and felt a lot of insecurity because of the fact that she had tried on numerous occasions to kill herself. She showed me her left arm and there were big deep scars from razor blade slashes, all up her arm, on the right arm too. It surprised me about Jenny that she was so warm and friendly, almost like someone I had known all my life as on the contrast, most of the others there were pretty stand-offish and not over friendly when they had learnt that I had come from prison.

I had to get a job and after a while I got one at Leyland Motors, the nearest main factory which I was to work at was at Zetland. So I applied for the job that they had there and got it. It was a 7 am to 3 pm job, working in the tyre and wheel alignment section. So I met some good people down at the "Park" some of whom had been there a long time, going back to the old days before the royal commission into Mental Hospitals. I think that the royal commission into Mental Institutions must have happened about the mid-fifties.

Nobby Clark was a good friend of mine and sometimes of an evening we would walk up to the TAB and have a couple of bets on the dogs or do a little bit of shoplifting maybe. (I am ashamed to admit it.) I started doing the shoplifting then with Nobby. We would grab anything that looked like "easy pickings". Nobby would come up with some good stuff like gold rings and watches but then he would get scared that he might have been spotted by a store walker or detective and he'd sell the stuff to me "cheap" like maybe for five or ten dollars for a pure gold ring or a Waltham gold plated wristwatch. Lots of times we'd go down to Paddy's Markets to do our shoplifting, but we'd never steal rubbish stuff that was of no use or not sellable. Another favourite lurk that Nobby and I loved to do was to stand around the cooked king prawn stand at the Fish Markets and when there was a good crowd around, well we'd just sidle up and put our arm through and grab maybe four or five huge freshly cooked king prawns. Then we'd go stand a fair distance away and eat our "spoils" and laugh about what cunning smart thieves we were. (God, have mercy on me!) It was all very enjoyable and we made a first rate team me and Nobby.

One day in Sydney, I was walking through the middle of town and while passing this music shop I happened to notice this second hand cornet for thirty dollars in the window, so I went in and after seeing that the instrument seemed to be in good working order and didn't have any of the parts missing, I gave the guy the dough and left the shop. The result was even to this very day I am a devoted cornet player. I used to sit on a seat down at Callan Park and practice and it didn't take me that long to get the hang of it either, though I never learnt to read music, I played entirely by ear. (There are some who think my playing isn't that good – but, to each his own opinion!)

Shoplifting – a five year setback

I never let up on the shoplifting, though something inside me must have been telling me to give it a miss, it wasn't right I was letting the Good Lord down!. But despite this, I kept on going into supermarkets like Franklins with my Army jacket on and would come out sometimes with my pockets bulging out with tins of imported Portuguese Anchovies in Olive Oil. I was very fond (as you may gather) of the anchovies. Sometimes I would go there a couple of nights in a week to make a "score". Well I got away with it for a considerably long time, but this particular night I got nabbed by this dame in Franklins. I must have pushed my luck there for too long.

So she had these two big muscularly "chocco" looking guys with her to back her up. So they grab me and are escorting me. We are walking down through the shop. They have hold of me and I can see that straight ahead of me there is a back door where the loading bay is. So I decide that I will make a break and run for it which I do.

Well they are taken pretty much by surprise but still I know that they are chasing after me so I make it easy to the loading bay, and jump down there and am down along the laneway and out and running straight across the road near to the Rozelle traffic lights.

The cars and trucks and buses are all screeching to a halt wondering, "Who in hell is this damned maniac?" (Yours truly) and "What on earth is going on?" But alas and alack! I am not in fit enough condition as an agile thief of this calibre should be, and the smoking habit, over the years has taken its toll. So I get about half way across the road when one of these "choccos" gets me in a flying tackle and his mate and this broad are pretty soon there as well, and this dame is yelling and screaming, "Hold him, hold him!" Every one for half a mile around is stopping and looking to see the comedy that is taking place there and just to get a "decco" at what is going on.

So this 'mother' with the big biceps who has brought me down is looking at me with this stupid gloating expression all over his kisser, and his kisser is right in front of me so I think to myself, "OK, Pal. Well, if I am going back to the Big Joint because of the likes of you, well here is a little going away present".

So I bring my fist back, bunch my knuckles as hard as I can and drive the lot right into this son-of-a-gun's nose with all of the strength I can muster. Splat! I feel the fellow's nose crack beneath the force of my fist and blood starts running out like somebody turned on a tap.

This determined chap cries out and grabs his schnoz and then the dame starts to scream out for help again. But I am too exhausted to run any more so I have to give in and allow them to take me into the back of the shop while this 'Sheila' phones for the police. They make me sit in a chair and then they sit there too to watch me till these couple of detectives arrive from the Balmain Station house. The detectives then proceed to charge me with shoplifting and the dame says, "And assault too, officer! Don't forget poor Frankie's nose".

Poor Frankie is still holding a handkerchief over his nose. This detective looks at the "chocco" and then says with a half-smile, "Yeah! Well we won't worry about the assault – that's a case of self-defence".

I said.

"Yeah officer, that's right".

But this broad won't shut up and she keeps on winging in this cop's ear every couple of minutes while he is trying to write out his report. Till at last the detective has to tell this 'Sheila', "Look! Do us all a favour and go home to your old man! Go on! Take a hike!" She looks real offended, but gets the message and shuts her yap.

She won't argue with this detective. So I tell them, "Yes I did take the stuff". Then secondly I say that I am already on license from Long Bay for 5 years, and then I tell them I am living down at Callan Park as an "Out-Patient" for the time being.

So then they ring up the ward to find out if this is true, and after talking to the charge nurse there at Ward 4–5, they tell me, "OK, Bob, you can go for now. If we need you, we will be in touch". I was going to reply, "Yeah, well don't hurry" but I thought that it might sound a bit cheeky, so I didn't.

So I go back to my little grey blanketed bed in the ward, and start to think how glad I am that I got off so lightly.

Well, a week or two passes and I am really starting to think that I won't hear any more about the shoplifting business so I am there sitting on the edge of my dormitory bunk practicing a few bars of "*Melancholy Baby*" on my cornet when in walk a couple of "Johnny Laws" from the Balmain Station House, and they tell me with no further ado, "Bob, you have got to come along with us". They have the "Bun Wagon" outside and I am told to get in, and we go first stop down to the Balmain Station House. But the worst part is that when they go inside the station, they leave me outside in the Bun Wagon and I am busting real bad for a "crap". Well after a while they came out. I am nearly crapping my pants, but no, "You'll be right Bob" and "Sit on it Bob, you'll be right, pal". I could've taken my pants off and done it on the floor, but I held on. So off we go back to the Bay, bump, bump, bump. Every bump we go over I think is going to be my last, but no "God is with me, or so it would seem. This will teach me to follow the Ten Commandments!" Pretty soon, "Thank goodness!" We roll into the front entrance at the Bay. Well, let me say right here, I have never been so relieved to get anywhere in all of my life, and I tell the screw in charge that they can throw the key away if they want to as long as I get to the "John" in time. So he lets me use the screw's one which is close handy. God's Truth!. I though it must be a near miracle that I made it in time.

Well here I am again and I couldn't care less. I see a lot of guys I know who are equally pleased to see me! Sensible guys not fruitcakes, so I'm glad that I am back and feeling about as much at home as my body can feel.

The screws are so pleased to see me back that they make me a trusty and put me to work outside the Prison – on the workers' gang, who are at this time working on building a whole new section of the prison wall, and the chief overseer screw who knows me says, "Hughie, here's all you have to do, mate. Just operate the hoist. Our old hoist operator lag gave out, so now we need a new one. Do you think you can handle it OK?"

I tell him, "Boss, I will give it my very best shot". So he said, "Great! You will need to give it a fair few trial runs to get the hang of using it, but the main thing is to stop it at exactly the right level so the wheelbarrow guy can wheel his load off easily". So I had to try a fair few times but after a while I felt I was accomplished enough and started work. There was a lot of mental concentration needed on this job and a lot of responsibility too, and I could see where men's lives (if you like) and welfare lay entirely with the fact that I did not get tired and fall asleep on this job. Wheelbarrow guys would go onto the hoist with their wheel-barrows laden down with new bricks or freshly mixed concrete. I would have to make sure that I stopped the hoist at just the right level, not too high and not too low.

It was a good job, but I couldn't describe it as easy. The concentration and responsibility here was too much for me. So I decided to ask the screw for a transfer to another job. I told the screw this and he said, "OK, Hughie, if that's what you want. I will try to find you a more suitable job".

Now the screw here must have asked around, because after a while, this Irish Catholic screw (Jerry C) that I knew, came and said to me. "Well, there is a good job there with me, if you want it, as an off-sider on the truck with me".

We had to deliver vegetables to the different kitchens and sections of the Prison. It was just the kind of job I wanted, and I could eat all the fresh fruit I wanted. Jerry knew I was a converted Catholic. That was why he gave me the job. He liked the idea of having another Catholic riding alongside of him. He didn't have much time for the "Bloody Protestants" and was always telling me so. He had been on a Pilgrimage to Rome twice with his wife. The lucky dog!

So Jerry and I worked together for a long while and a better boss I never had. I used to "gig" him a bit about working for the "crown". He didn't mind. He would say to me, "Well, I've got to bloody well eat too, haven't I?"

I started to paint again while I was in there for those extra four or five years and did quite a lot of good completed works of art. Lots of them were later stolen, I think. In any case, they went somewhere along the course of time. I don't know where. This young lady (a 'you beauty' Sheila) used to come in and tutor us in different ideas in art. She was married, but we didn't mind. I sent several of my paintings into the "Art Shoppe" where works by prisoners were sent to be sold, but I don't know what happened to them! I never saw them again.

My grandfather used to do some very creative oils and water-colours, so I suppose I had the gift from him.

Freedom?

I had to front this head-shrinker every so often. His name was Dr B, a small slight fellow, not very old, with spectacles, long hair and a girlish, kind face. He took a very keen interest in me right from the word 'go'. I used to be called around to see him about once a fortnight continually. I don't know whether or not he was a Catholic himself, but when he heard that I had turned to the Church myself, and was attending regular Mass, he seemed all the more anxious to help me. The idea of it must have made a real good impression on him.

Then it wasn't too long after, and after I had assured him that I had sincerely learnt my lesson as to the utter 'stupidity' of the shop-lifting spree that he agreed to help me obtain another five year license. – This all happened after I had been back in the "stir" for another four and a half years.

Then I was visited by Dr Paul Lush, who, acting as ago-between for the 'Mother of God Brothers', asked me if I would like to go and live with them for the duration of my licence.

I said, "Yes, I would".

So he then informed the Brothers that I had said that I was interested and they sent one of their number, Brother Denis Devcich, to interview me and "check me out", so to speak, to see what kind of a person I was.

Well, Brother Denis was a quietly spoken bloke and after we had talked a bit, he said, "Well, OK, Bob. I'll see if I can make arrangements for you to come down and meet the other Brothers".

I found out after, that the Brothers lived in a large place at Pott's Point, which had been rented to them by the Sisters of Charity.

Brother Denis pretty soon fixed it up and soon thereafter, I was told to dress in my good clothes and a couple of Detectives had been given the authorisation to take me down to Pott's Point and meet the rest of the Brothers.

The First Brother I saw was a lean looking Brother who met me standing on the front steps of 'Guadalupe House'. This was Brother Mark Sheehan, and after shaking his hand, I soon found that he wasn't such a bad bloke to have as a friend. I didn't expect that. – Well then I was led into meet Brother Michael Foran. Brother Michael was a small, chubby, pleasant fellow who took me at face value and said that he thought that I would probably "fit in" all right if given the chance. Brother Michael, I found out later, was the founder of this group of Brothers.

So I was then told I would be released into the custody of the Brothers who had just taken possession of a large house, a former Orphanage, just out of Albury. I had never been south of Sydney, except when I had been a prisoner in Goulburn Gaol, so I didn't know what to expect.

I was taken to Mascot Aerodrome one morning and made myself ready to go to Albury by Fokker Friendship via East-West Airlines. This I did and the trip was quite comfortable and only took one hour. They even served me coffee and fruitcake on board the aircraft.

When I arrived at the airport at Albury, I was met by Brother Robert McNally, who was about as friendly as I could have expected under any circumstances, and who made friendly conversation with me till we reached the newly rechristened 'Guadalupe House' where the Brothers now lived and where I once again met Brother Michael and Brother Mark.

I met other Brothers too, who were members of the Community and who helped me to put in the five years very happily in serving out my licence.

"Institutionalisation Syndrome"

But don't anyone have the idea that it was easy for me to adapt to civilian life again after having been a crim behind bars for so long. The abrupt change brought on a kind of a feeling of "nausea" which only left me after a point where my re-adaptation to society was complete. For a long while, this "nausea" feeling was like what a fish from the ocean might have when it is taken from its natural environment and made to live among human beings in an aquarium. It had me, sometimes at a point where I was just a hair's breadth away from heaving a brick through a jewellery store window, or some such caper, in order to be taken back inside gaol. But I am pleased to be able to say that I am good at sticking things out, so I did stick it out and after a while, the "nausea" feeling left and I was OK once again. One would have to experience something like it to realise just what it was like and how hard it was to conform. But I did have help (from God and from my friends, the Brothers and others). I appreciate that fact too.

As I write, I still live here in Albury and I must thank the Mother of God Brothers, who did not really know me or what kind of a person I was on the inside, but still put a lot of trust in me and took me at FACE VALUE and lived out the Gospel according to Christ's word in so doing. But I appreciate that they did something here for me that was entirely out of human charity. That is not a very common thing in a world that lives by grabbing everything for itself, and where the law of the jungle and the animal kingdom seems to reign supreme.

I also have to thank my friend, Dr Paul Lush, and the people of Albury themselves who have been friendly to me since my coming to live here.

Last of all, I wish to thank my dear cousin, Fay for never giving up on me after what I did, but she stuck staunchly by me. She truly proved that blood is thicker than water and showed the essence of true Christian love. Her love for me must be greater than I deserve.

Postscript

This is the end of my story, written as true as I can recall it.
R.J. Cox